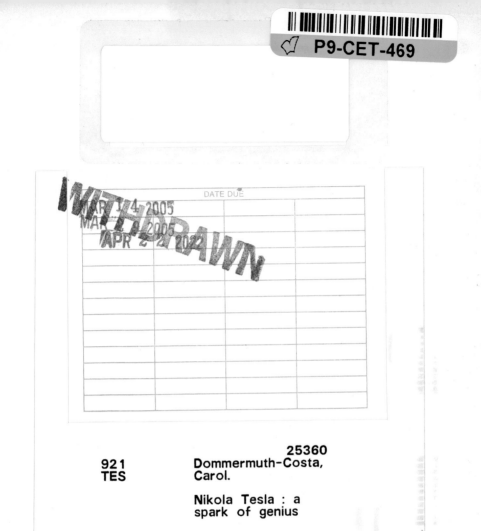

25360

921
TES

Dommermuth-Costa,
Carol.

Nikola Tesla : a
spark of genius

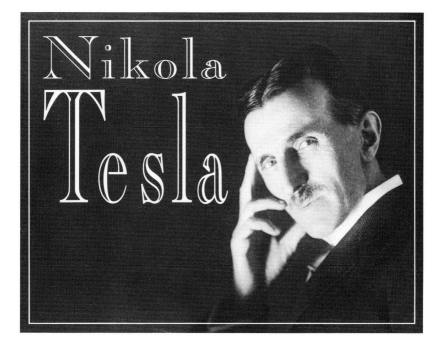

Nikola Tesla

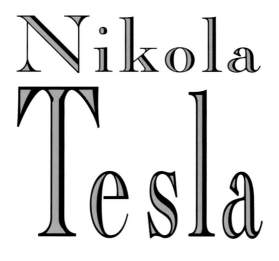

 *A Spark of Genius*

Carol Dommermuth-Costa

LERNER PUBLICATIONS COMPANY · MINNEAPOLIS

I would like to thank the following people who generously gave of their time and knowledge and who supported and encouraged me during the writing of this book: Dr. Ljubo Vujovic—a man dedicated to making Nikola Tesla known to the world, who introduced me to the right people; Nicholas Kosanovich, president of the Tesla Memorial Society, who generously made volumes of Tesla material available to me; William Terbo, Nikola Tesla's grandnephew, for his patience in answering my questions and verifying information; Dr. Bollinger at the University of Buffalo, an expert on the scientific aspects of Tesla's work, who graciously took the time to answer my questions regarding scientific matters; Dr. Marincic, the curator of the Tesla Museum in Belgrade, for his generous time spent digging up photos for this book; my editors at Lerner, Becka McKay and Dawn Miller, who spent many hours refining and polishing this book; my dear friend Maria Lagonia, who first put me on the right path of research; and Chris McGovern, for his love and encouragement during the writing process.

Library of Congress Cataloging-in-Publication Data

Dommermuth-Costa, Carol.
    Nikola Tesla : a spark of genius / by Carol Dommermuth-Costa.
        p.   cm.
    Includes bibliographical references and index.
    ISBN 0-8225-4920-4
    1. Tesla, Nikola, 1856-1943—Juvenile literature. 2. Electric engineers—United States—Biography—Juvenile literature.
3. Inventors—United States—Biography—Juvenile literature.
[1. Tesla, Nikola, 1856-1943. 2. Electric engineers. 3. Inventors.]
I. Title.
TK140.T4D66   1994
621.3'092—dc20
[B]   93-43123
                                                                CIP
                                                                 AC

Manufactured in the United States of America

1 2 3 4 5 6 – I/JR – 99 98 97 96 95 94

To my children,
Danielle and Jeffrey—the light in my life

Contents

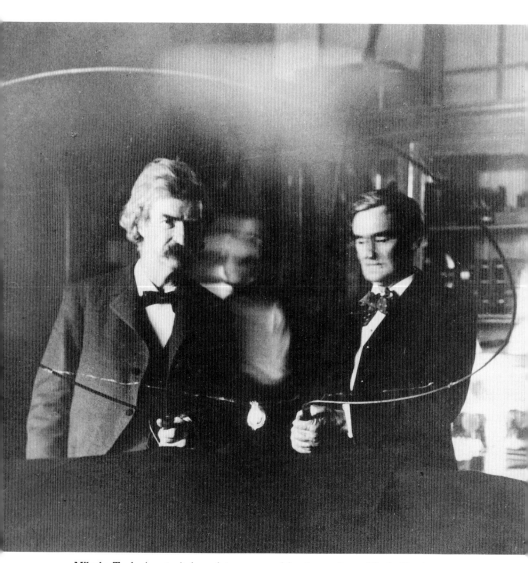

Nikola Tesla (center) *loved to amaze friends such as Mark Twain* (left) *and actor Joseph Jefferson* (right) *with experiments in electricity.*

ONE

A Child of the Light

1856–1863

Ten o'clock in the evening approached as Nikola Tesla hurried back to his lab after dinner. His guests would be arriving soon and he didn't want to be late.

Neighbors watched Tesla with lowered eyes as he walked past them and entered the dark stone building in lower Manhattan. As usual, they could hear the lock being clicked into place after Tesla went inside, and as usual, they thought that no good was going on behind that door. But a locked door was not the only cause for neighbors' suspicions. They frequently saw and heard frightening things coming from inside the lab.

Sometimes, late at night, Tesla's neighbors would be awakened from a sound sleep by thunderous explosions that would actually shake their beds. Startled residents would run to their windows to see if the lights were on in Mr. Tesla's lab—was it Tesla or an earthquake that had caused the tremor?

If anyone had peeked through the cracks in the boards covering the windows of Tesla's lab, they might have seen gigantic streaks of light shooting through the room as if an electrical storm were taking place indoors. And in the middle of this lightning storm they would have seen a dark-haired gentleman sitting calmly in a chair as if nothing unusual were happening.

Dramatic spectacles were common in the lab of Nikola Tesla. He was a scientist and an inventor, and his passion was electricity.

On this particular night, Mr. Tesla had invited a few friends to his lab. He was going to demonstrate the results of some of his latest experiments. Most of his guests had just arrived.

But where was his friend Samuel Clemens? As Nikola Tesla looked at his watch, he heard a loud knock on the door. Tesla opened it, greeted his old friend warmly, and showed him to his seat. Nikola regarded the handful of people in the room. They all looked as if they were awaiting a performance in a theater. Well, he was about to give them a show they would not quickly forget.

Tesla waited until his audience was quiet. He then walked up to a wooden platform in the front of the huge cavelike room. Built under the platform was a generator capable of creating millions of volts of electrical current. Tesla stepped onto the platform and turned to face his friends.

Within seconds, cries of astonishment broke the silence in the room. Tesla's body was surrounded by wild streaks of lightning. More than two million volts of electricity were hitting Tesla, lighting up the air around him as if he were a neon sign. While his friends sat staring in wide-eyed astonishment at this spectacle, electricity appeared to pulse from Tesla's body in all directions. Moments later he jumped off the platform apparently unharmed, yet observers could still see fine threads of light surrounding his body and clothing.

Nikola Tesla was once called an "electrical wizard," and his demonstrations seemed like magic acts to a public uneducated in the properties of electricity. While Tesla spent most of his life craving solitude, he also enjoyed his role as a performer. With his striking looks—straight black hair and piercing blue eyes—he was perfect for the role. He liked watching the looks of amazement on the faces of his spectators, knowing that he was both entertaining and teaching them at the same time. When Tesla left his audience, however, he was once again a scientist and inventor of the utmost seriousness.

The study of electricity was serious business to Nikola Tesla. He saw unlimited possibilities for the world, if people could learn to harness and use this natural force. He dedicated his life to learning more about it.

Nikola Tesla was born at midnight between July 9 and 10, 1856, in Smiljan, a small village in Croatia. On the night of Nikola Tesla's birth, a fierce thunderstorm was raging over the village of Smiljan. At the precise moment of his birth, the sky lit up with a huge bolt of lightning. The midwife who had just delivered the new baby turned to Nikola's mother and said, "Your new son is a child of the storm."

Nikola's birthplace in Smiljan, Croatia

Nikola's father, Milutin Tesla

Mrs. Tesla responded by saying, "No, he is a child of the light."

Although Nikola was born in the nation of Croatia, his parents, Milutin and Djuka (pronounced DOO-kuh) were originally from the nation of Serbia, on the border of Turkey.

Milutin, Nikola's father, was a well-educated priest of the Serbian Orthodox Church. When Milutin was a young man, his father decided that Milutin should be a soldier like himself and the other men in the family. But Milutin had other plans. He informed his father that he was determined to enter the priesthood and nothing could make him change his mind. Milutin's father, seeing the determined look on his son's face, finally agreed.

Milutin was a philosopher and a fine writer and poet. He had an incredible memory and could recite poetry and prose in several different languages. He had a strong and disciplined mind, and he tried to teach young Nikola how to strengthen his own mind. Milutin would recite a poem only once, asking Nikola to concentrate on the words and then recite it back to him.

Sometimes Milutin would give Nikola difficult mathematical calculations to do. Nikola was not allowed to use a pen and paper but was required to complete the calculations in his head. This mental discipline helped Nikola in his work as a great electrical scientist.

Nikola's mother, Djuka, was also intelligent and talented. Because she spent her youth helping to raise her six brothers and sisters, she had no formal schooling. But Djuka taught herself to read, and Nikola always saw a book in his mother's hand whenever she had a few minutes to herself. She especially

Nikola's oldest sister, Angelina Tesla

loved poetry, and she memorized hundreds of poems, not only from her native Serbia, but from all over the world. Serbian poetry, when recited in the Serbian language, sounds very musical. Nikola would hear his mother recite poems over and over again as she did the household chores.

Djuka's life was not easy. She not only took care of her husband and five children, she also managed their small farm. Djuka often invented useful tools that could save her a little time or labor and make her work easier. She transformed simple items found around the house or farm into parts of new inventions.

Invention was familiar to Djuka. She had come from a family of inventors. Both her father and grandfather had several inventions to their credit, and Djuka inherited their talent. Nikola often marveled at his mother's ability to create new implements out of scrap material. He often said that his mother, more than anyone else, influenced his life as an inventor.

Nikola himself displayed an inventive mind as early as age five, when he made his first invention. One morning Nikola was invited to go fishing with his brother Daniel and some friends. One of the neighborhood boys had found a hook and some other tackle, and the excited boys set out for the local pond to go frog fishing.

While the other boys headed to the far end of the pond, Nikola decided to remain by himself. Here, he thought to himself, he could fish in peace. The other boys were always so noisy they chased all the frogs away. But then he realized he didn't have a hook!

Nikola took a piece of wire and pounded it into a hook using two stones. He then attached the hook to a string, gathered some bait, and went to a part of the brook where he knew there were lots of frogs. But he had no luck.

Nikola was getting discouraged when it occurred to him to dangle the hook in front of a frog that was already sitting on a tree stump. This idea worked and soon Nikola had caught several frogs.

Nikola never suffered from a lack of ingenious ideas. His mind was almost always working on a better or more efficient way to make things work.

One unique idea was a motor powered by june bugs. June bugs were so abundant in Croatia they were considered pests. Sometimes they would even break the branches of trees with their weight.

Nikola decided that these bugs could be put to use. He designed a crosspiece made out of two sticks of wood and to this he attached a large wooden disk. He then glued as many as four bugs to this device. When the june bugs fluttered their wings, they would cause the disk to rotate with considerable speed. They would continue for hours, increasing their speed with the heat of the day.

Nikola had planned further experiments with the june bugs, but a hungry stranger intervened. A boy from another village had wandered over to see what Nikola was doing. When the young inventor's back was turned and his attention was absorbed in making adjustments to his bug-motor, the boy devoured a handful of june bugs from Nikola's private stock. Nikola turned around in time to witness the boy's mouth stuffed with june bugs. Sick to his stomach, Nikola ran home. He was never able to touch another insect again.

Although Nikola had friends in his village, he enjoyed his times of solitude. During these important moments alone, ideas and inventions would pop into his head. Sitting in the woods or on the bank of a pond, Nikola constantly observed the ways of nature. Even at this young age, he believed in an important connection between the natural world and human-kind. He felt that if people could learn to understand nature's secrets, there would be no end to human accomplishment.

In 1863, when Nikola was seven years old, his older brother, Daniel, was killed while riding the family horse. The Reverend Tesla thought that moving away from the house that now held such a painful memory would be good for the family. When he was offered a post in a Serbian church in the nearby town of Gospić (pronounced Gospich), he readily accepted.

Nikola was crushed by the thought of leaving his home. He would miss the long walks in the woods that he was so familiar with. He would miss sitting and thinking by his favorite pond. He would be in the city. Instead of tall trees, he would see nothing but buildings.

When Nikola was seven, his family moved to the town of Gospić, where he attended the Real Gymnasium.

At first Nikola was bored in Gospić. He felt like a prisoner in his new house. All his friends were back in Smiljan, and he was too shy to make friends with children in the new city. During the first week, the only time he went out was to go to the service at his father's church.

Then one Saturday the Tesla family was invited to join the other townspeople for a picnic and a celebration. The town leaders were very proud of some new and advanced firefighting equipment. After many speeches, a demonstration was announced.

People waited patiently while some strong young men began to demonstrate the new pump and hose. The equipment was to be operated with water from the nearby river. But when the apparatus was finally in place, not a drop came from the hose.

The town officials stood in an embarrassed silence, not knowing what to do next. Suddenly, Nikola jumped into the river with a huge splash. Once under the water he swam directly to the hose and straightened out a kink that had formed in it, allowing the water to flow freely.

Everyone cheered, and his father turned to him and asked, "Nikki, how did you know what was wrong with the hose?"

Nikola replied, "It just came into my head and I knew what I had to do." The cheering continued, and the firefighters carried him through the town. At the age of seven, Nikola was a hero.

TWO

A Mind of His Own

1864–1870

Daniel Tesla's death had upset each member of the family in a different way, but young Nikola perhaps felt most profoundly affected. He became unusually preoccupied with the thought of death. Night and day he would think about it and shiver with fear. The many sermons that he had heard from his father's pulpit about the devil and a fiery afterlife surely added to his distress. Soon after Daniel's death, Nikola began to experience many strange visions.

One morning Nikola awoke to see the first of a recurring set of images dancing in front of his eyes. People, places, and things that he had seen in the past all came into view. Sometimes these pictures were so clear that they almost completely blocked out his ordinary vision. He became confused about whether he was seeing something real or something imaginary. Often, just a word from someone could set off these images, and once they started, they were difficult to stop.

Nikola was a little frightened by these strange occurrences and decided to tell his older sister Milka about them. Sharing his problem with his sister was a relief. They talked about a possible solution. Milka didn't know any more about what was happening to Nikola than he did, but she helped him in another way. During the times he was seeing these images, she would verify for him whether or not they were really present or

Nikola's sisters, Milka (left) *and Marica* (right)

whether they were just visions. Milka's support helped calm Nikola's anxiety about what was happening to him. Now he could think more clearly and try to find a way to deal with this unusual situation.

Nikola began by pushing his mind beyond what he thought its limits were. As he suspected, the images gradually began to change. No longer did he see only familiar objects and places. Now he saw new scenes.

> These were at first very blurred and indistinct, and would flit away when I tried to concentrate my attention upon them, but by and by I succeeded in fixing them....

These scenes gradually became stronger and clearer and Nikola finally began to see them in solid form.

>I soon discovered that my best comfort was attained if I simply went on in my vision farther and farther, getting new impressions all the time, and so I began to travel—of course, in my mind. Every night (and sometimes during the day), when alone, I would start on my journeys—see new places, cities, and countries....

Nikola would have to wait several years before he could gain enough power over his mind to rid it of an unwanted image. Only with a strong act of will would he eventually succeed in getting the images under control.

Once the family had settled in Gospić, Nikola was enrolled in school. The local school—called the Normal School—was about the same as the second through fifth grades in the United States.

Nikola enjoyed school and was a good student. Not many of the other students had Nikola's capacity for learning, nor did they come from families who considered learning an important part of the day, as the Tesla family did.

When Nikola was 10 years old, he graduated from the Normal School and entered the Gymnasium in Gospić. This school was the equivalent of an American junior high school.

Attending school at the Gymnasium opened up a whole new area of interest for Nikola, primarily because there were many mechanical devices at school with which he could experiment. Models of water turbines—devices with rotors turned by water—especially intrigued him. When Nikola was about five years old, he and Daniel had made a simple model of a water turbine in the pond near their home, and the concept had fascinated him ever since.

Nikola was looking through some books in his father's library one day. One book had photographs of interesting places around the world. One photo in particular made quite an impression on Nikola's young mind. The picture showed millions of tons of water cascading with tremendous force over a sheer wall of rock. The photo was of Niagara Falls, located in upper New York State on the Canadian-American border.

As a child, Nikola saw a picture of Niagara Falls and became fascinated by its power.

Nikola thought Niagara Falls was a terrible waste of water. He wondered if a turbine could be built that could generate some kind of power using this water. Nikola put this idea in the back of his mind. Maybe he could think about it later.

The teachers at the Gymnasium were proud of Nikola for his scholastic achievements. He excelled in all his subjects, especially foreign languages and mathematics. Nikola had recently decided that he wanted to be a scientist, and he became even more dedicated to his studies. All the thoughts and ideas that now passed through his mind were far more creative and inventive than ever before.

In order to rest his busy mind, Nikola would read novels and write poetry. He especially liked to read at night when the rest of the house slept. It was quiet and there was no one to tell him that he was going to hurt his eyes from reading so much.

When Nikola was about 12 years old, his father came into his room one night and found him reading in the dark with only the light of a candle. The next day, all the candles were taken away and hidden so Nikola couldn't find them. The Reverend Tesla did not do this out of meanness. He was simply afraid that his young son would ruin his eyesight forever.

Nikola was momentarily frustrated, but his inventiveness helped him find a solution: he made his own candles. He then stuffed rags into the crack under the door so the light in the room would not be detected by his parents. Nikola could read all night and slip into bed just before dawn, when his mother rose to begin her chores.

Nikola was constantly looking for ways to improve himself. After reading *The Son of Aba,* a novel by a leading Hungarian author of the time, Nikola decided that he was going to make some changes. He felt that he, unlike the hero in the book, lacked willpower and discipline. He decided to deny himself things that he wanted most, in order to develop self-control.

Nikola was anxious to begin his lessons in self-discipline, and the next day in school he had his first opportunity. His mother had given him a favorite fruit with his lunch. When lunchtime came, he took it out of his pocket, anxious to bite into it. As he looked at the fruit, he realized that to deny himself this treat would help him master his impulses. So he offered the fruit to a classmate, who savored it while Nikola looked on.

Although he longed for the fruit, Nikola was proud of himself for exerting self-control. Nikola believed that the success of his future life would depend on having certain qualities. A disciplined mind and lifestyle would give Nikola the stamina he needed for a lifetime of hard work.

Even as a teenager, Nikola was very aware of the tremendous power of nature. One winter day, Nikola and some friends took a hike in the mountains. Fresh snow had fallen, and the boys set about making snow sculptures and snowballs. The snow was powdery, so most of the snowballs didn't get too big. But one snowball did. The boys watched in awe as their small snowball grew larger and larger, gathering speed as it rolled down the mountain. It became so enormous that it took not only snow but also trees and soil with it. When it finally reached the bottom, the snowball landed with a thunderous drop that shook the mountain. Nikola and his friends were lucky. If the snow at the top of the mountain had loosened when the mountain shook, it would have started an avalanche that could have killed them all.

Nikola learned a valuable lesson that day. Nature had tremendous power, and something as insignificant as a snowball could release a powerful force under the right conditions. This experience left an unforgettable impression on his mind.

In 1870, when Nikola was 14 years old, he was ready to graduate from the Gymnasium. He had excelled in all his classes and his parents were very proud of him. When he received his grades just before graduation, however, he was surprised to discover that his mathematics teacher had failed him for the year. Nikola was shocked. All of his test scores had been very high. Why had the teacher decided he deserved to fail the class?

Nikola immediately made an appointment with the director of the school. He told him that he thought the math grade was unfair. The director, however, took the side of the teacher.

Nikola politely suggested that perhaps the teacher had confused him with another student. He asked to be retested. Nikola insisted that the director make up the test himself, and that it be very difficult and cover everything Nikola had learned in mathematics. He would prove that he deserved the highest grade, not the lowest one.

The director could not refuse his appeal. Nikola took the test and received an almost perfect grade. The director was astounded. He apologized to Nikola and to his parents and adjusted the grade.

Soon, news of Nikola's mature way of handling the situation in school became well known in the small city of Gospić. As a result, Nikola was offered a job in the local library, reviewing and cataloging all the books.

Nikola carried out his duties as diligently as he did everything else in his life. This was an exciting job. He had already read almost all the books in his father's library. Now he could read all the books in the public library as well.

Sometime after he started his job, though, Nikola became ill. The illness started when the Reverend Tesla told his son that there was no reason for him to enroll in the Higher Real Gymnasium, since he was going to be a minister. The Higher Real Gymnasium in Karlovic (pronounced KAR-loh-vich) was the next formal school that Nikola would enroll in if he were going to continue his studies. Comparable to an American high school, the Higher Real Gymnasium prepared students for the university. Nikola had planned to continue his education so that he could fulfill his dream of being a scientist. But what could he do when his father insisted that he become a minister? How could he disobey him?

Nikola's sadness began to affect him physically. He lost all his energy and his appetite. Even his job at the library did not excite him anymore. The librarian had sent a huge stack of books to Nikola's house so that he could work on them, but they sat on the floor, untouched.

The thought of not being able to spend his life discovering and inventing depressed Nikola deeply. The doctor sighed in despair. He told Nikola's parents there was nothing physically wrong with their son. He had lost his will to live.

One day the mail carrier brought a letter addressed to the Reverend Tesla. It was from the reverend's cousin in Karlovic. In her letter, the cousin asked if Nikola could stay with her while he was attending the Higher Real Gymnasium. She had assumed that he would be going. When Nikola's father read the letter, he decided it was a sign from God that Nikola should continue his education—at least for a while longer.

As soon as Nikola heard the good news, he began to recover. There was so much to do before he left for Karlovic.

Nikola at age 19

THREE

Decisions to Make

1871–1877

In September of 1871, 15-year-old Nikola arrived in Karlovic. He had a few days to relax before he was to begin his first semester at the Higher Real Gymnasium. His relatives were happy to see him and welcomed him into their home. Their own children had grown up and moved away. It eased their loneliness to have a young person in the house again. Reverend Tesla had written to them about Nikola's illness, so his cousin took it upon herself to see to Nikola's health. She believed that a person in delicate health should be very careful about what he or she ate and, most important, should not overeat. Based on this theory, she gave Nikola very small portions to eat and refused to give him more food even when he asked for it.

Nikola was always hungry. He often thought longingly of his mother's delicious meals and the heaping portions she served. He was homesick, and had it not meant leaving his studies, he would have gone home. He decided to work extra hard, take additional courses, and finish his studies as soon as possible. Then he could leave Karlovic and return home.

Nikola's plan worked. By June of 1874, at the age of 17, he had completed a four-year program at the Higher Real Gymnasium in three years. He had one of the highest averages in his class. Nikola had also made a firm decision about his future.

He knew that he wanted to be a scientist, but now he also knew which field he would concentrate on. Thanks to a dynamic professor of physics who had made a deep impression on his young student, Nikola decided to devote his life to the study of electricity.

Nikola was anxious to share his decision with his family, so he began to pack for his return trip home to Gospić. Before he could leave, however, he received a letter from his father that contained an unusual message. The Reverend Tesla told Nikola to go on a hunting trip before he came home. Nikola knew that his father was adamantly opposed to hunting, so he was puzzled by this strange request. He soon found out, however, that a cholera epidemic was spreading throughout the town of Gospić. Nikola's parents were afraid that if he found out about the epidemic he would want to come home and do what he could to help. They did not want him to be exposed to the disease.

Medical science of the time had not yet discovered the cause of cholera. Several residents of Gospić had already died of the disease, which caused severe diarrhea and dehydration. The people didn't know they should stay away from the polluted water that carried the disease. As a result, the epidemic was spreading rapidly.

Nikola was not to be stopped from going home. He wanted to surprise his parents with the news of his decision to become an electrical scientist. He wanted to see their pride when he told them he had graduated with high honors. But the Reverend and Mrs. Tesla had a surprise for their son. They were angry. Why hadn't he obeyed his father? Did Nikola think he knew better than his parents what was good for him?

Nikola's father made a decision for his son's own good. Seeing how tired and drawn his son was, the Reverend Tesla finally decided that the academic environment was too stressful for Nikola's delicate health. Another reason for him to enter the clergy! The Reverend Tesla was insistent. Nikola's school days were over.

For the second time in his life, Nikola lost the will to live. His depressed mental state and his worn-out physical health made him prone to illness. His weakened body was not able to fight off germs, and he contracted cholera.

Nikola became critically ill. His family had little hope of his recovery. The Reverend Tesla was overcome with grief at the thought that he might lose a second son. Lying ill in bed, Nikola whispered to his father that, if he were able to look forward to a career suited to his talents and ambitions rather than the ministry, he might rally and get better.

Suddenly, the Reverend Tesla remembered a similar scenario from years earlier, when he had persuaded his own father to let him become a minister instead of a soldier. He saw that his son must be allowed to follow his own path in life. The Reverend Tesla told Nikola that he could pursue a career in electrical engineering and promised to help pay for his education. Nikola was grateful for his father's blessing, and his family watched with relief as he made a speedy recovery.

In April 1875, 18-year-old Nikola's dream had come true at last. He was preparing to go to the city of Graz in Austria to continue his technical education at the Polytechnic Institute. His excitement mounted as the first day of school approached.

But as luck would have it, he received a notice that he was to be drafted into the army. The law required all young men at the age of 18 to give some time to military duties.

Even though the Reverend Tesla was aware of this requirement, he was very upset. What if Nikola was killed? He couldn't bear to lose another of his children.

The Tesla family had many members in important positions in the military. Nikola's father could probably use his influence to keep Nikola out of the army. But until this was taken care of, Nikola had to leave town for a while and hide out somewhere. On instructions from his father, Nikola packed some clothes, books, and writing materials and set off for a hunter's cabin in the nearby mountains. He was told to remain there until he was sent for.

Nikola's stay in the mountains was a very fruitful period for him. He had time to rest and strengthen his body. He also had the privacy and solitude he needed to read, write poetry, and work on preliminary designs for some of his new inventions.

Meanwhile, the Reverend Tesla had several meetings with relatives who held high posts in the military. He made them aware of his son's fragile health and they decided to excuse Nikola from military duty. Several months passed. Finally the paperwork was completed and Nikola could return home.

In September 1875, at the age of 19, Nikola was ready to begin his first semester at the Polytechnic Institute. Now his real training in engineering would begin.

Nikola was determined to work exceptionally hard at his studies so that his father would not regret the decision to let him study at the institute. Nikola kept to the commitment he made. He set a rigid schedule for himself and determined to follow it each day.

The room where Nikola slept was not heated during the night, so the only warmth was under the covers. Most of the students hated to get up in the morning because the air in the rooms was freezing and the bare floors seemed even colder.

But Nikola faithfully rose from his warm bed every morning at 3:00 so that he could study before classes.

His studying went far beyond what was required by his professors. He spent all of his free time in the library studying instead of being outdoors, something that he had always enjoyed. His friends encouraged him to go out and have some fun. They teased him by telling him that too much studying would make him dull and boring. Nikola would only smile and shake his head. With his books tucked firmly under his arm, he would stroll off to the library or the lab.

Nikola's drive to excel in his studies allowed him little time to develop the social side of his personality. When his friends were dating and going to parties, Nikola was usually studying in his room or in the library, or just lying on his bed thinking of ideas for new inventions.

Nikola was afraid to get involved in any kind of romantic relationship. He feared that this kind of commitment would take too much time away from his studies. From the comments that his friends made, he believed that the only thing on the minds of young women was marriage. Nikola couldn't think about marriage for a long time, if ever. He had to give all his energy and time to his work.

When Nikola returned home for a short visit, he was greeted with the usual praise from his mother, but was dismayed by the lack of praise from his father. After all, he had sacrificed much of his time and worked more diligently than most students. Why wasn't his father overjoyed to see how well he had done?

What Nikola didn't know was that a member of the Institute's teaching staff had contacted Reverend Tesla to express concern about Nikola. The professor had noticed how relentlessly Nikola was pursuing his studies—sometimes even forgetting to eat or sleep. The professor feared that if Nikola didn't slow down a bit, he would surely drop dead from exhaustion. After hearing this, his father decided that if he refused to make a fuss over his son's scholastic success, Nikola would be discouraged and cease to pursue his studies in such a determined manner. Nikola was puzzled and hurt by his father's reaction, but he continued to push himself in his studies.

Since he was such a brilliant student, Nikola was allowed to concentrate his energies in mathematics, mechanics, and physics, to the exclusion of most other subjects. His class in physics was especially stimulating. Professor Poeschl (PUSH-ul) was a man with many degrees in his field, and he was held in high regard by colleagues and students. Although students joked about the fact that he came to class in the same wrinkled suit day after day, Professor Poeschl performed experiments with a precision that his students admired. They would never think of questioning his judgment.

The institute had the good fortune to obtain a new motor and the students were very excited to have this machine in their classroom. Everybody was talking about it. The American inventor Thomas Alva Edison had designed it for the purpose of generating direct-current electricity. This machine promised to provide light so that people could work and play during the darkness of the evening.

Professor Poeschl was anxious to demonstrate the motor to the class. He explained that this motor, designed by the brilliant Mr. Edison, was the only one of its kind. It would make it possible to someday use direct current to light up homes and cities.

Thomas Edison (seated) *made many innovations in the field of electricity. The dynamo* (below) *used direct-current electricity to generate power.*

The professor went on to say that *alternating* current, however, was useless, since it could not be generated. Several scientists both in the United States and Europe had already tried unsuccessfully to build an alternating-current motor.

Nikola, who had been paying attention to every word, had an intuition. He told Professor Poeschl that he believed it possible to design an alternating-current motor.

Professor Poeschl's face turned red. How dare this student assume to know more than the great Mr. Edison. He must not let his other students think that this kind of behavior would be tolerated.

"Mr. Tesla may accomplish great things in his life," he admonished. "But he certainly will never do this. It is an impossible idea!"

Nikola was embarrassed at first. But he was a young man who had confidence in his own mind and his own judgments. Deep inside he felt that he was right. The idea only needed some ironing out, and that would come in time. Meanwhile he would go on with his studies and let the idea take deeper root in his mind.

Current and Voltage

One way of explaining current and voltage is to compare it to water moving through a pipe. Current is the *amount* of water flowing through the pipe. Voltage is the *force* of the water that you would feel if you held your hand over the end of the pipe.

Direct Current and Alternating Current

Direct Current

The electric current produced by a battery is an example of direct-current electricity. Electrons flow from the negative terminal to the positive terminal of the battery. Because the charge of these terminals remains constant, the electron flow (current) goes in one direction only. Individual electrons move slowly, but when the electrons of a conductive material (such as a metal wire) are charged, loose electrons shift rapidly from one atom to the next, producing a rapid electric charge.

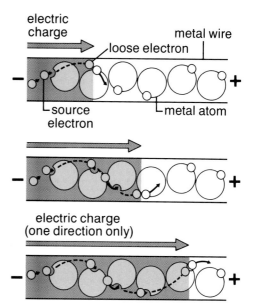

electric charge (one direction only)

Alternating Current

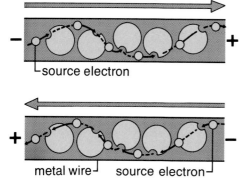

With alternating-current electricity, the source terminals change repeatedly from a negative to a positive charge, and vice versa. The change causes the electrons to move back and forth rapidly, changing direction 60 times a second and thus alternating the direction of the current flow.

Nikola spent one year in Prague, studying science at the University of Prague.

FOUR

On His Own

1878–1881

Nikola's studies at the Polytechnic Institute were completed successfully, and he was supposed to begin classes at the University of Prague in September. But he decided to wait a year. Nikola knew that his parents were making a great sacrifice to send him to school. He thought that if he worked for a year and saved his own money to pay for his tuition, he wouldn't be a burden to them.

Nikola found a job in the city of Maribor, near Graz. He earned about 60 florins a month, which was a good wage in 1878. He lived very simply in an inexpensive boardinghouse near his job, and he saved his money for school. By September of 1878, Nikola had saved enough money to pay for his first semester at the University of Prague.

Although he had felt a great deal of satisfaction at his job, the university was the place where Nikola felt most comfortable. Here he had access to the labs and all the equipment for his experiments. He also loved being in an atmosphere of knowledge and learning. He loved the books, libraries, and professors. Now he could start testing some of the ideas that were burning in his mind, and he would begin by trying to design a motor that could generate alternating current.

In the year 1878, direct current was still the only usable form of electrical current. But Nikola felt certain that direct current was a limited and ineffective source of power. He strongly believed that future technology would demand great amounts of electrical power. Direct current was weak—it would not be able to meet the demands of a growing world. Direct current could be generated only for about a mile, and then it would begin to lose energy. A city would need to install hundreds of generators just to power its lights. This was impractical and expensive.

Nikola believed that alternating current, on the other hand, was a more effective and less costly method of generating power. Unlike direct current (DC), alternating current (AC) could generate high voltages for long distances without growing weaker. Transformers would then reduce the high voltage for safe use in people's homes. The cost of building numerous direct-current generators would be eliminated. Yet no one had been able to design an alternating-current motor that worked.

Nikola had not forgotten his experience in Professor Poeschl's class. He still believed that a motor could be designed that would generate alternating current. But how could it be done? Nikola decided to devote all his time and energy to finding out.

He began by constructing one machine after another in his mind. Because of Nikola's unusual powers of visualization, he could actually see the machines in his mind and work on them without ever drawing a diagram or building a model.

> I started by first picturing in my mind a direct current machine, running it and following the changing flow of the currents. Next I would visualize systems comprised of motors and generators and operate them in various ways. The images I saw were perfectly real and tangible.

After many long months of pondering the problem, Nikola was no closer to a design of an alternating-current motor than before. But he didn't give up. He was convinced that there was an answer. He just needed more time. Meanwhile, his year at the University of Prague was almost completed. When he wasn't working in the lab or on class assignments, Nikola continued to think about how to build his AC motor.

During the summer after Nikola's first year at the university, the Reverend Tesla died. He had left a small savings for Djuka to live on, but Nikola and his sisters now had to support themselves. This meant that Nikola could not continue at the university. He would have to find a job.

A friend of the Tesla family told Nikola about the Central Telegraph Company in Budapest, Hungary, which was hiring men with backgrounds in electricity to work on a new project. Nikola decided to go to Budapest and apply for a job.

When he arrived in Budapest, Nikola expected to be hired as an engineer, but he found that the project was still in the planning stage. There was little need for an engineer with Nikola's qualifications.

He was disappointed and uncomfortable. He had traveled so far, and now the only position the company could offer him was that of draftsman. He was obviously overqualified for the job, and it paid a fraction of the money he expected—but it would be enough to survive.

In spite of his initial disappointment, Nikola made a commitment to his work and did the best he could. His diligence paid off. The inspector chief soon noticed that Nikola was capable of a more responsible position. Nikola was given a new job that involved designing a new telephone apparatus. This would satisfy his creative and inventive mind and also pay more.

Nikola was grateful for the recognition and worked long hours, resting only three hours a night and sleeping two. He had an unusual amount of energy. There just weren't enough hours in the day to accomplish all that he wanted to do.

Eventually, though, the poor sleeping and eating habits caught up with him. Nikola became very sick with a mysterious illness.

Doctors were called in and shook their heads after examining Nikola. One doctor told Nikola that it was the strangest sickness he had ever seen. The doctor feared he would not be able to cure it.

Twitchings and tremors racked Nikola's body continuously, causing him much discomfort. His nerves became overly sensitive, and for the second time in his life Nikola began to experience unusual things.

Nikola had this portrait made in 1882, around the time he solved the puzzle of the alternating-current motor.

> ...I could hear the ticking of a watch with three rooms
> between me and the time-piece. A fly alighting on a
> table in the room would cause a dull thud in my ear.
> The sun's rays...would cause blows of such force on
> my brain that they would stun me.

The ground seemed to tremble continuously, and Nikola had to put rubber cushions under the legs of his bed in order to get any rest. Moreover, the heat of the sun also caused him great pain. In the dark, he had the sensitivity of a bat. He would get a peculiar sensation in his head when he came within 12 feet of any object. Nikola didn't have to see it, he could "sense" it.

Another doctor was called in. He prescribed a common medicine of the day, but he knew that it probably wouldn't help. He didn't think Nikola was going to make it.

But Nikola desperately wanted to live. He had so much left to do. The puzzle of the alternating-current motor was almost solved. He felt that he was on the brink of a solution, but he needed more time.

A friend of his, Anital Szigety, convinced Nikola that the road to health lay in fresh air and exercise.

Anital told his friend that he was working too hard. If Nikola didn't exercise his body as well as his mind, he'd be so sick that he wouldn't be able to work.

This made a lot of sense to Nikola. His work had consumed all his energy and time, and he had ignored his own health. Every day Anital would visit Nikola and the two men would go for walks.

One day Anital and Nikola decided to walk through the local park in Budapest. Nikola was feeling much better thanks to Anital's help. His strength and energy were returning, and he sensed that in no time he would feel normal again.

*After leaving the University of Prague in 1879, Nikola found a job
in Budapest.*

The sky was clear on this particular day and the air was
comfortably warm. The two friends had stopped walking long
enough to enjoy the sight of a flock of birds vying with each
other for a few crumbs of bread that a passerby had thrown
on the ground.

Nikola had told Anital before the walk that he was going
to give his mind a rest. He decided not to think about the
alternating-current motor until the next day. Anital thought
this was a great idea. Now that Nikola's body had rested, his
mind could rest as well.

Instead of discussing electricity and mechanics as they
usually did on their walks, Nikola recited poetry to Anital. Some
of his favorite lines were from *Faust,* a German play.

The glow retreats, done is the day of toil;
It yonder hastens, new fields of life exploring;
Ah, that no wing can lift me from the soil
Upon its track to follow, follow soaring!

Nikola had no sooner finished reciting these lines, than he abruptly stopped. His eyes were glazed and he seemed to be in a kind of trance. Anital panicked, thinking that Nikola was having a relapse of his sickness. He began to shake his friend, hoping to snap him out of his strange mental state.

But Nikola was not ill, nor was he in a trance. In fact, he was so happy at that moment that he was unable to speak. He had come upon a solution to his alternating-current motor!

Grabbing Anital's arm with one hand and a twig with the other, Nikola forced his friend to kneel on the ground with him. He drew a diagram in the dirt as he explained to Anital the concepts he had just discovered. His intuition had again revealed a secret to him—the solution that he had been looking for. Not only did he now have the means to construct an alternating-current motor, he also had discovered a new scientific principle.

Nikola knew that when an electric current is generated, a magnetic field is also created. He now realized that there was a way to transform this magnetic field into a whirling, rotating force. This could be done with the use of an armature, which would create two or more alternating currents out of step with each other. More electricity would be generated than with direct current, and for a longer distance. Nikola finally saw a way to make possible what Professor Poeschl had called impossible.

Nikola found Paris to be an exciting and cosmopolitan city.

FIVE

The Land of Golden Promise

1882–1884

In 1882, Thomas Alva Edison, a young inventor and entrepreneur in New York, saw the potential for expanding his business in Europe. He knew that Europeans would soon want to do away with their old-fashioned telegraphs and welcome the more modern telephone. So Edison decided to open a smaller version of his company in Paris to prepare for the new communications network that he was sure would take Europe by storm. It was here, at the Continental Edison Company, that Nikola would apply for a job.

In Budapest, Nikola had tried, and failed, to excite people with talk of his new discovery. But he had higher hopes for Paris, the city of writers and artists—all open-minded people! Surely he could find someone in Paris who would be excited by his ideas.

Twenty-six-year-old Nikola arrived in Paris ready to begin working at the Continental Edison Company, his head full of ideas for numerous types of alternating-current motors. It had been almost all he could think of since the previous year in Budapest when he had made his discovery. In his mind's eye, he could see all the parts of the machine, completely real in every detail.

In less than two months, he had mentally created and tested every type of motor that would later be patented in his name. But Nikola needed money to build these alternating-current motors and show the world their great potential. He grew almost dizzy with excitement when he thought of the tremendous effect this discovery would have on people's lives. Large factories could be powered with electrical machines instead of mechanical ones. Whole cities could be lit up with only one generator instead of hundreds.

Nikola, unlike some scientists and inventors with a new discovery, was not secretive about his ideas. He didn't wait until he filed a patent before talking about his discovery. Nikola felt that scientific discoveries didn't belong to any one individual—but to the whole world. So he told everyone in Paris who would listen, hoping that someone would believe in his idea enough to lend him the money to build his motors.

Unfortunately, Nikola didn't have to worry about anyone stealing his idea because no one believed him. Everyone listened with polite attention, but they thought Nikola was being hasty, speaking as if his alternating-current motor had already been tested.

One possible backer told Nikola that when he built an AC motor and proved that it could work, then maybe he would help Nikola with some money. Nikola protested that he needed money to build a motor and he didn't have any. The man replied that he couldn't afford to invest in daydreams.

Disappointed but not discouraged, Nikola began working at the Edison Company in Paris. His job was to travel around Europe to power plants that were in need of repairs. On one of his assignments, he was sent to Alsace, a small region on the French-German border. A railroad station lighting plant had malfunctioned during an event meant to celebrate its installation. The German government was furious with the Continental Edison Company, which had installed the lighting.

Promised a huge monetary bonus when he returned to Paris, Nikola was sent to Alsace to find and repair the damage. As Nikola worked at the railroad station, he thought about the motors he would be able to build with the extra pay he would earn.

But Nikola was impatient. He was anxious to get started on his motor. He had brought some materials with him from Paris, and a man in the town where he was staying offered Nikola space in his mechanical shop. Now, when he wasn't working on the power plant for the Edison Company, he could start to put his motor into physical form right there in Alsace.

Working on something of his own was so rewarding that Nikola often became completely absorbed in what he was doing. All of his specifications and measurements for the AC motor were in his head. He concentrated intensely on his work. And Nikola was a perfectionist. Every part had to be polished, attached, and adjusted down to the finest detail before he would continue. Once built, the actual motor was almost identical to the motor that he had carried around in his head for so many months.

The next step was to test the motor and see if it worked. Nikola constructed a dynamo (a machine that changes mechanical energy to electrical energy or vice versa) to generate the alternating current to the motor. If the motor turned when he flipped the switch, his theory would be correct. If nothing happened and the armature didn't move, then he would have to admit that he had wasted many months of his life in idle daydreams.

Nikola flipped the switch. Immediately the armature began to turn; at first, slowly, then in a few seconds it was spinning at full speed. Nikola then flipped the reversing switch and the armature performed just as he had envisioned. It stopped

Induction Motor

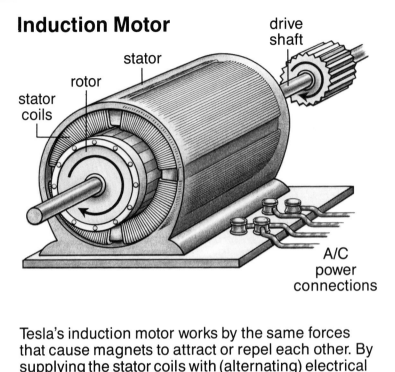

Tesla's induction motor works by the same forces that cause magnets to attract or repel each other. By supplying the stator coils with (alternating) electrical energy, a magnetic force field is created that in effect "rotates" around these stationary coils. This magnetic force causes the rotor, positioned inside the coils, to be "dragged" to follow this rotation. As the rotor turns, the drive shaft connected to the rotor also turns, resulting in an output of mechanical energy.

An electric generator, or dynamo, uses the same process as a motor, but in reverse. Mechanical energy (rather than electrical) turns the drive shaft and rotor, resulting in an output of electrical energy. In a hydroelectric turbine, for example, rushing water is the mechanical energy that eventually creates electricity.

momentarily and started turning in the opposite direction. Here was the proof he needed. It worked!

Now he had an actual working motor to demonstrate to the public. Nikola was sure that everyone would soon come to see its great potential and practicality. Meanwhile, he worked hard to finish his assignment at the railroad station. He was anxious to return to Paris, collect his bonus, and start building his motors.

As soon as the job in Alsace was completed, Nikola took the next train to Paris. He went directly to the office to collect his pay, but there was nothing for him. Nikola appealed to one of the administrators of the company who lightly shrugged off

A model of Nikola's alternating-current motor

Nikola's concern and directed him to another executive for approval. When Nikola approached this executive, he was given the same line as before and sent to a third executive. This man told Nikola to go back to the first administrator.

By this time, it was obvious to Nikola that he had been cheated—after all of his long hours and hard work! And what was worse, he had as much money now as before—none.

Nikola was angry. He felt that he had been taken advantage of, and now, without any money, he couldn't build his motors. He didn't bother going back to the first administrator. He went instead to his table to pack up his belongings. He was quitting the company.

One of the managers of the company, Mr. Batchelor, learned of Nikola's situation and felt sorry for him. He knew that Nikola was not only a brilliant engineer but also a dedicated worker. He thought of a way to help him.

Batchelor urged Nikola to go to New York and get a job with the parent company, directed by Mr. Edison himself.

Batchelor gave Nikola a personal letter of introduction. He instructed Nikola to tell Mr. Edison that he was sending Nikola to him with highest recommendations. He also warned Nikola not to let Edison turn him away before reading the letter. Edison had a reputation for being very abrupt at times.

Nikola didn't take long to decide. A few days later, in June 1884, 28-year-old Nikola had bought his tickets, and with a few possessions packed, he arrived at the railroad station ready to board the train. When he reached into his pocket for his train ticket, however, he found his tickets and his money gone. He never knew whether a pickpocket had stolen them or whether in his haste and excitement he had dropped them, but there wasn't time to think about it. Running alongside the moving train, Nikola jumped aboard with his small valise in his

Charles Batchelor (above) *was impressed by Nikola's scientific brilliance and recommended him to Thomas Edison* (right).

hand. If he didn't get to America now, he might never have the opportunity again.

The small change in his pocket paid for his train fare, but he didn't know how he was going to get on the ship without his ticket. When Nikola reached the dock where the *Saturnia* waited for passengers to board, he explained to the captain that he had lost his ticket. The captain saw that one berth had not been claimed, so he gave it to Nikola. It was, of course, the berth that Nikola had paid for with his lost ticket.

As the ship sailed, Nikola sorted through his few possessions: a notebook of poems he had written, some mathematical calculations that he was working on for a new invention,

When Nikola arrived at Ellis Island (above) *in New York Harbor, New York was bustling with immigrants from all over Europe* (opposite).

articles he had written on the subject of electricity, and about four cents. Four cents in 1884 was worth more than it is now, but it still couldn't buy very much. Despite having so little money in his pocket, Nikola felt fortunate. He had a letter of recommendation to work for one of the greatest inventors of the time, Thomas Edison.

When he stepped off the boat in New York, Nikola watched businesspeople approach the other immigrants with job offers. These men had railroads and buildings to construct. They were looking for cheap labor, and what better place to look than the docks, where poor, often desperate immigrants would take any job offered to them. Nikola felt luckier than his shipmates. He had both a job prospect and an invitation to stay with a friend in New York for a few days until he could get settled.

Cab fare was more than four cents, so Nikola started walking to where he would be staying. He looked at everything, trying to drink in his new and foreign surroundings. Nikola looked up to the sky and saw wires endlessly criss-crossing each other: telegraph, telephone, and electrical wires all hanging from wooden poles, forming what looked like a spider's web in the sky.

Nikola was jolted out of his thoughts at the sight of a store owner angrily kicking a machine that was sitting in front of his shop. When Nikola asked what the problem was, the

man told him that it had never worked properly and he had worn out his patience in trying to fix it. Nikola offered to give it a try.

Within half an hour, Nikola had repaired the machine. The store owner stared in disbelief as its motor hummed. He immediately handed Nikola a twenty-dollar bill and offered him a job. Nikola thanked him for the offer, replying that he hoped to have a job with Mr. Edison. The store owner said that Edison could use a good man like Nikola. Edison was always having problems with his electrical wiring, and he didn't always have enough good engineers to work with him.

Unfortunately for Edison, the man's words were true. Thomas Edison was an inventive genius, responsible for developing direct current, inventing the incandescent lightbulb, and installing electric lights in many of the expensive homes in New York. In 1881 the Edison Electric Light Company was commissioned by the city of New York to install tubes, wires, conductors, and lampposts throughout the city. Edison also built the first electric lighting station, which became one of the wonders of New York. But Edison still had to contend with many problems.

Edison's engineers were sometimes not as careful with their work as they should have been. Fires were a perpetual problem. If the engineers did a poor wiring job in a building, its walls would later catch fire. Also, the Edison generators were not as efficient as they could have been. They frequently needed repairs. This was how things stood when Nikola Tesla was directed into Edison's office early one afternoon in 1884.

Edison had just received a message that there was a fire in one of the most expensive homes in New York, the Vanderbilt Mansion. Apparently, the electrical wires that his company had recently installed had ignited, and a fire had started

The first Edison electric lighting station in New York

inside a wall. All of Edison's engineers were out on other jobs so he would have to go see to it himself. He was just about to leave when he received another emergency message. The oceanliner *Oregon,* loaded with passengers, had been ready to sail for Europe when its lights went out. Apparently, the dynamos that Edison's company had installed for the lighting plant on the ship had problems right from the start. Now they had completely shut down. The captain of the *Oregon* was furious. Edison had better send someone over there immediately, or else!

Now what was he going to do? The fire couldn't wait, but neither could the *Oregon,* which had a schedule to keep. As Edison pondered the problem, his secretary led Nikola into the room and made introductions.

Edison snapped that he had no time to hear Nikola's story, but Nikola handed him the letter of recommendation from Mr. Batchelor. Edison momentarily forgot the emergencies as he read the letter in his hand. Batchelor stated in the letter that besides Edison himself, Nikola was one of the greatest men he'd ever known. But Edison was unconvinced. He told Nikola that Batchelor's saying so didn't make it true. Nikola would have to prove it to him. If Nikola was willing to start right away, Edison would give him a chance to live up to Batchelor's words. He told Nikola about the problem on the *Oregon* and walked out the door.

Nikola took the tools he needed and headed for the docks. When he arrived, the captain was waiting impatiently. He started yelling at Nikola at once. How could Edison send only one man? The captain needed the job done today, not next week!

Nikola politely informed the captain that he was the only man available for the job and assured him that the ship would be able to sail the next morning.

With help from a few members of the crew, Nikola began to repair the dynamos. He worked all night and finished at 5:00 the following morning, just in time for the ship to sail, as he had promised. Nikola assured the captain that the lighting equipment would work better than ever.

Exhausted from his labors, Nikola walked back to Edison's shop in the early morning hours. As he approached the building he met Edison with two other men. They were just leaving the office.

With his usual sarcasm, Edison remarked, "Here is our Parisian, walking around all night"—implying that Nikola had been out all night socializing. He was quite shocked when Nikola responded, "No, sir. I've just come from the *Oregon*. Both your dynamos are repaired."

Edison walked away without saying another word. He never gave compliments directly, but Nikola heard him say as he walked away, "That is a darn good man Batchelor sent me."

Nikola had a job!

Nikola at age 34

SIX

Battle of the Currents

1885–1890

For the next year, Nikola worked unusually long hours. His day began at 10:30 in the morning and he would continue working until 5:00 A.M. the next day. Around 8:00 P.M. he would stop for a light dinner. Edison appreciated the time Nikola put into his job, because Edison also worked long hours. It was common knowledge that he slept only two hours a night, although his employees often found him taking naps during the day. Both Edison and Tesla were full of energy and sincerely dedicated to their work.

But the similarities between Edison and Tesla stopped there. They were actually very different men in personality and work habits. Nikola was polished and well-educated, with a gentle, quiet manner. People felt calmed by his presence, never doubting that they were with a great man. Edison was also recognized as a man of genius. But unlike Nikola, he hadn't graduated from high school or college. Edison had gained his knowledge through practical experience. He could be difficult, often brusque, in his manner of dealing with people, and he was sometimes boisterous in public. He had an astute business sense, though—something that Nikola did not have.

The differences in the habits of these two great men became a problem when they had to work near each other. Nikola was clean and neat, sometimes to the extreme; Edison was

sloppy about himself and his workplace. This was difficult for
the fastidious Nikola to accept. After walking into Edison's
office, Nikola would often ask himself how anyone could work
in such a mess. On the other hand, Edison thought that Nikola
was too much of a perfectionist and too neat.

Edison also thought that Nikola was too caught up in his
"ridiculous" alternating-current scheme. When Nikola first
told Edison about his AC motor, Edison laughed in his face.
He told Nikola that direct current was the only system he
would ever use. He also predicted that there was no future
in alternating current and that anyone who gave it any attention was wasting time. Edison told Nikola that if he wanted to
continue with this "alternating-current nonsense," he should
do it on his own time.

After Nikola had been working for Edison for several
months, he noticed that the dynamos that generated electricity for Edison's lighting plants could be improved to work
more efficiently and economically. Nikola approached Edison
with a proposal. If he could improve the dynamos, would Edison give him a bonus? Nikola thought that with this money he
could set up a lab of his own. Edison not only agreed to the
bonus, he recklessly told Nikola that he would give him $50,000
if he could improve the dynamos.

Nikola worked for months on the project, sleeping and
eating very little. He took no time for himself, dedicating all
his time and energy to the project. He didn't mind working
hard because he knew that he would soon have enough money
to build his motors and experiment with some of his own
ideas instead of someone else's.

The day finally came when Nikola walked into Edison's
office to announce that he had finished designing as many as
24 types of dynamos, and that the machines that he had al-

The first Christmas tree lit by incandescent lightbulbs, which were invented by Thomas Edison.

ready built worked beautifully. Nikola asked for his money as promised.

Edison merely smiled. "Tesla, you don't understand our American humor," he said, turning his back on Nikola and walking out the door.

Nikola had been cheated again! Angry and frustrated, he stormed out of the office, never to return.

No one really knows why Edison made this idle promise to Nikola. Some think he recognized Nikola Tesla's genius and knew that if the young inventor had financial independence, he might successfully compete with Edison. Others think Edison wanted to keep Nikola as an employee in order to prevent him from developing the alternating-current system. Perhaps Edison didn't think it was as ridiculous an idea as he let on. Still others think that it was not unusual for Edison to break promises that way.

Twenty-nine-year-old Nikola was now on his own. But with very little money in his pocket, he couldn't do much more than look for a job. Then, a few months later, some financial investors—people who wanted to put their money into a profitable business—approached Nikola. They knew of his reputation as one of the finest electrical engineers in the country, and they told him that they wanted to form a company in his name. Nikola was ecstatic! Finally, someone who believed in him. Here was the financial backing he needed to further develop his AC system.

The Tesla Electric Light Company was formed in 1885. Nikola was promised shares of stock in the company. He was given a laboratory on Grand Street in New York City. He could finally work on some of his own designs, Nikola thought. But his financial backers had other plans for him.

In 1885 the new arc light was being used to light the streets of New York City. But the arc light was impractical. It used too much electricity and was therefore expensive. The officers of Nikola's company wanted him to work on improving the arc light. Their intention was to sell this newly improved light and make a fortune. Nikola was told that this project had to come first, and then he would be given money to do his own research.

After several months of work, Nikola developed a new arc lighting system. This lamp was safer, more reliable, and more economical than the original. Nikola's investors were happy and so was he. Now he could go on with his own work, or so he thought.

Nikola found that the money for research, which was plentiful when he was working on the arc lamp, was suddenly cut back considerably. He was told that he was no longer needed in the company. Nikola felt cheated again. The investors had used Nikola's talent for their own profit and then driven him away when they had what they wanted. Nikola was out of a job once again!

The year 1886 was a difficult one in New York City. Money and jobs were scarce. The only work to be found was hard labor. With no job and no means of support, Nikola had to dig ditches at the wage of $2 a day in order to survive. This was the most difficult period of Nikola's life. He felt as though all of his education and all of his abilities were being wasted. He became very depressed. His dreams of having his own laboratory now seemed as far away as his native Croatia.

After months of this labor, the supervisor of the work crew introduced Nikola to Mr. A. K. Brown. Mr. Brown was the manager of the Western Union Telegraph Company. He knew about alternating current, but unlike Edison, Brown believed that alternating current had great potential. He had heard of Nikola's work in the field of electrical engineering. He also knew that Nikola had successfully built and tested an AC motor. Here was a genius with a mind overflowing with new engineering advances, and he was digging ditches!

Brown put a stop to that immediately. He loaned Nikola money to cover his living expenses for a while. Then he formed a new company in Nikola's name—the Tesla Electric Company. Brown told Nikola that he could have his own lab and his own time, on one condition. Nikola had to continue his research into the development of the alternating-current system. Nikola couldn't believe he was hearing these words. His dream had become real after all.

Nikola's laboratory in New York

As soon as a laboratory was rented on Fifth Avenue in New York City, Nikola got to work building various electrical machines. Since he had already worked out the problems in his mind, he was able to produce these units very quickly. All of the designs that had been resting inside his head since the breakthrough he had in Budapest could now be constructed. Although several years had elapsed since that day in the park with his friend Anital, he remembered the designs down to the last detail. Nikola had spent much time testing the designs in his head, and they all worked exactly as he had anticipated.

He designed motors with various functions, all using alternating current. He constructed dynamos for generating the current, transformers for adjusting the voltage, and devices for automatically controlling the machines.

Nikola's ideas were completely new to the field of electrical science. In the years 1887 and 1888, Nikola applied for and was granted more than 30 patents for original work. This was unprecedented in the Patent Office. No one inventor had ever produced so much original work in such a short time.

Suddenly the world of electrical engineers began to take notice of Nikola Tesla. In 1888 the prestigious American Institute of Electrical Engineers invited Nikola to give a lecture

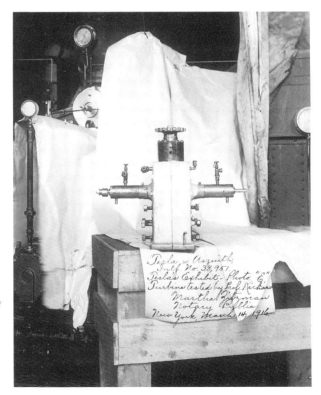

An early Tesla turbine

on his work with the alternating-current system. He accepted
the honor and took a great deal of time to prepare his speech.

Nikola was a very humble man. He didn't speak of his
own work. He spoke of Michael Faraday, who in 1831 discovered the existence of electrical current. He spoke of other
great scientists of the late 1800s who had contributed so much
to the world with their discoveries and inventions. Finally, he
spoke about the great technological advances that were possible using one of nature's gifts—electricity.

Nikola smiled with pride when the engineers rose from
their seats and applauded him at the end of his speech. The
events of this evening firmly established Nikola Tesla as the
father of alternating current and a true genius in the field of
electrical engineering.

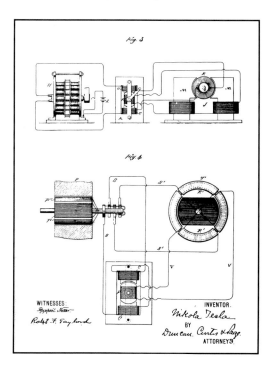

One of Nikola's patents
for the alternating-
current motor. A
patent is a form of
protection for an
inventor. An inventor
sends diagrams and
precise descriptions to
the U.S. Patent Office
in Washington, D.C.,
where it is put on file.
This ensures that no
one else can claim the
idea as theirs.

Michael Faraday discovered the existence of electric current.

As Nikola's name became known and his work with alternating current became more accepted, the public became divided into two opposing groups. Some people, like Edison, believed in and trusted direct current and didn't want any changes. Others, like Nikola, could see the potential of a new system. The "battle of the currents" had begun.

Opinions were voiced in newspaper letters and editorials. Politicians found that this topic was hotter than any current political issue, and they debated it whenever possible. Wealthy entrepreneurs and businesspeople also entered the battle.

Edison set up a campaign against the alternating-current system. He took advantage of the uninformed public. Most people did not have enough technical knowledge to make an educated judgment about either AC or DC. They based their judgments on emotion. So Edison criticized AC to whomever he met, praising the virtues and potential of the DC system. People believed Edison. After all, many people had never heard of Nikola Tesla. He had gained recognition only recently with other electrical engineers. Edison made a promise to the public. He told them that soon, after he had ironed out all the wrinkles in the direct-current system, there would be no need for any other system. He told them that alternating current was dangerous and even lethal. Surely they could not feel safe having it in their homes.

Backers of the Tesla system were not as harsh as Edison. They tried to convince the public that the AC system had the potential to improve their lives because it could generate far greater power than the direct-current system could, and in a safer, more economical way.

Everyone was confused. Whom should they believe?

In 1889 Nikola received a guest at his laboratory. The guest was George Westinghouse, a wealthy and astute businessman from Pittsburgh. He was the inventor of air brakes for railroad trains, as well as many electrical devices. He was also Edison's competitor and a major player in the battle of the currents. Westinghouse had learned of Nikola's achievements in the field of electricity and had wanted to see for himself what this electrical genius was like.

The two men liked each other immediately. Westinghouse felt right at home in Nikola's lab. Here was a room filled with transformers, dynamos, and motors of every conceivable type. Westinghouse, in his best suit, got down on his hands and knees

George Westinghouse (right) *became a good friend to Nikola and one of his most important investors.*

to examine the machinery in detail. He moved switches, he pulled, he prodded, he poked. He was astounded by the volume of work that Nikola had successfully completed. Westinghouse wanted Tesla on his side, and nothing would stop him.

Westinghouse offered Nikola $1,000,000 in cash, plus royalties, for the patents on his AC motors. (Royalties meant that each time the Westinghouse Company sold one of Nikola's motors or inventions, Nikola would receive a percentage of the profits. Nikola could be paid for the rest of his life, or for as long as the company was in business.) Nikola was taken aback, but he remained calm. This time he wanted to see it in writing. He told Westinghouse that he would accept the offer, but he needed a contract.

They had a deal. The two men shook hands. Nikola couldn't believe that this was happening. Should he trust Westinghouse to keep his word? In a few days, true to his promise, George Westinghouse delivered a contract and a check for $1,000,000 to Nikola's lab.

Westinghouse wasn't finished. He asked Nikola to work for a year in Pittsburgh, where his company was located. He told Nikola that he would be paid a generous salary if he would work as a consultant to his engineers.

Nikola spent most of 1890 in Pittsburgh, but it was a year of frustration. Although he had designed the motors, the engineers continually questioned and argued with him about the capabilities of the machinery. Finally, Nikola could take it no longer. He felt that he was wasting his precious time and accomplishing nothing.

George Westinghouse tried to persuade Nikola to change his mind. He even offered him a larger salary to stay on in Pittsburgh. But Nikola Tesla, now financially independent, refused. Westinghouse respected his decision and they remained friends for many years. Nikola was always grateful to Westinghouse for believing in him when others didn't. George Westinghouse was grateful to Nikola for his contribution to electrical science and to his company.

A Tesla coil

SEVEN

The Age of Invention and Electricity

1891–1893

There were great things going on in Nikola Tesla's lab in the 1890s. Nikola was now a wealthy man, thanks to the contract he had signed with the Westinghouse Corporation. He could work on his own inventions in his own time. He was happy. There seemed to be an unlimited supply of ideas in Nikola's mind. To him, the word "impossible" did not exist.

One of the first inventions Nikola completed in his new lab was an apparatus called a high-frequency alternating-current transformer—popularly known as the Tesla coil.

A transformer is a device that transforms or changes voltage and current. Some electronic devices require a high voltage in order to operate. The high current that is usually generated with this voltage is dangerous, however. The Tesla coil could change a low voltage to a high voltage with a safe low electrical current. Nikola knew that his transformer would become more and more necessary as people began to develop devices that used electricity. All modern electronic equipment—including televisions, radios, and stereos—requires a high voltage with a safe low current. These devices all contain some form of the Tesla coil. The Tesla coil is considered one of Nikola's most important contributions to modern technology.

Nikola thought of the year 1891 as one of the most important years of his life. On July 30, 1891, at the age of 35, Nikola became a United States citizen. He considered his citizenship more significant than any medals given to him by the scientific community.

Also in 1891, Nikola gave his second lecture before the American Institute of Electrical Engineers in New York. Here he demonstrated phenomena that the scientists had never seen before: electrical sheets of flame produced by huge Tesla coils; wireless electric lamps; and motors that ran on only one wire—something unheard-of in the 1890s. Nikola went so far as to suggest that in the future, motors would run without wires, drawing their energy from the atmosphere.

In 1891 Nikola gave a lecture to the Institute of Electrical Engineers in New York City.

Nikola (left) *performing an experiment with his good friend Robert Underwood Johnson*

Nikola also told the engineers that he had begun to work with X rays. His designs, along with the work of the German scientist Wilhelm Röntgen, led to the invention of the X-ray machine that still helps doctors save lives.

Few scientists had ever accomplished as much as Nikola had in such a short time. The world wanted to know more about the man and his inventions. His work was being discussed by every electrical scientist and inventor in the world.

In this experiment, Nikola's body conducts the electricity that lights up the glass tube in his left hand.

Universities and electrical organizations—both in the United States and in Europe—invited him to speak about his achievements. Nikola accepted most invitations, but he found traveling to so many lectures exhausting. Most of the invitations were from universities in France and England, and Nikola had to cross the Atlantic Ocean by steamship many times.

Unfortunately, even when Nikola returned home from these voyages, he didn't have much time or much privacy. Nikola had become so famous that everyone recognized him. He found that it was almost impossible to even dine alone anymore. "There's the famous Mr. Tesla," people would whisper to one another in a restaurant, pointing to Nikola's table.

Nikola's desire to be alone extended to his relationships with women. At the age of thirty-six, Nikola Tesla was an imposing figure. He was more than six feet tall and quite thin. Yet he was a strong man, with large hands and unusually long thumbs. (It was thought by many that a long thumb was a sign of great intelligence, and in Nikola's case it seemed to be true.) Women were naturally attracted to this dark, handsome, and intelligent man, but Nikola would not offer affection to any of them.

By the time he was thirty-six years old and had not yet married, society began to question Nikola's bachelor status.

Although Nikola was often encouraged to find a spouse, the handsome inventor was never interested in marriage.

No one could quite grasp the fact that Nikola wasn't interested in marrying. Eventually, scientific journals, such as the *Electrical Review* of London, joined the gossip columnists in their campaign to get Nikola Tesla married. The *Electrical Review* published an editorial about Nikola:

> ...whatever may be the cause of the abnormal condition in which this scientist finds himself, we hope that it will soon be removed, for we are certain that science in general, and Mr. Tesla, in particular, will be all the richer when he gets married.

Nikola, however, stood firm in his resolve not to get involved in a love relationship. When a reporter for the *New York Herald* newspaper asked Nikola if he believed in marriage for artistic persons, Nikola answered:

> For an artist, yes, for a musician, yes; for a writer, yes; but for an inventor, no...an inventor has so intense a nature...that in giving himself to a woman he might love, he would give everything, and so take everything from his chosen field.... It's a pity too, for sometimes we feel so lonely.

Nikola Tesla had decided that only with freedom from family responsibilities could he achieve great things.

Although Nikola preferred his own company at meals, he did sometimes accept invitations to parties and dinners at the homes of some of New York's high society people. Rich matrons saw the tall, handsome inventor as a lucky catch for their daughters.

Nikola was not interested in courting any of these women. There was one woman, however, whom Nikola was thought

Robert Underwood Johnson and his wife, Katharine, were good friends of Nikola's. Some people think Nikola may have been in love with Katharine.

to be in love with. Her name was Katharine Johnson, and she was the wife of Robert Underwood Johnson, a poet and the editor of *Century* magazine. Nikola met the Johnsons in 1893 and became close friends with the couple. Nikola was often invited to their home, where he met writers such as Rudyard Kipling and Helen Hunt Jackson, as well as artists and society people. A relaxed friendship developed between Nikola and the Johnsons. They would send each other notes by messenger, sometimes two or three times a day.

Nikola always hid his feelings for Katharine because she was married and the wife of his friend, yet many believe that she was the only woman who was ever able to touch his heart. Katharine, likewise, seemed to have deep feelings for Nikola that would come out in some of the letters she sent him. But Nikola knew there could be nothing more than friendship between himself and Katharine. He maintained his close friendship with the Johnsons until their deaths.

But could any woman have been happy, married to Nikola Tesla? The inventor had many phobias and eccentricities that would have tried the patience and understanding of anyone.

> I had a violent aversion against the earrings of women but other ornaments, as bracelets, pleased me more or less according to design. The sight of a pearl would almost give me a fit but I was fascinated with the glitter of crystals or objects with sharp edges and plane surfaces. I would not touch the hair of other people except, perhaps, at the point of a revolver. I would get a fever by looking at a peach....I counted the steps in my walks and calculated the cubical contents of my soup plates—otherwise my meal was unenjoyable. All repeated acts or operations I performed had to be divisible by three and if I mist [missed] I felt impelled to do it all over again even if it took hours.

Nikola was also disgusted by overweight people and finicky about women's attire. His female secretaries could expect to be sent home to change their clothes if Nikola didn't like what they were wearing.

Eventually, the many months of travel, lectures, dinners, and parties took a toll on Nikola's health. He became very ill.

He was in Croatia at the time, visiting his sister Angelina. For several weeks, he was confined to his bed, where he could do nothing but read and think. Volumes of poetry surrounded his sickbed and his notebook lay open beside them. Nikola began to write poetry again, just as he had done many years ago.

One day, as Nikola was deep in thought, he began to take a good look at his lifestyle during the past few months. He realized that he had devoted many hours, days, and weeks to making his work known to the public—but he hadn't created anything new. This apparent waste of his time disturbed him.

He confided to Angelina that he was through with giving his time to the world. Now he would take it back again. When he returned to good health, there would be no more hours wasted frivolously. Nikola needed to work!

When he returned to New York several weeks later, Nikola kept the promise he had made to himself. Invitations to dinners and parties continued to arrive but were sent back unopened. Universities still asked him to lecture but he declined the honors, saying that he was in the middle of an important project and couldn't leave. His lab was a haven where he spent long hours every day, sometimes talking to no one except his assistant.

The materials needed to build devices such as this Tesla coil were expensive, and Nikola often had trouble finding people willing to invest money in his projects.

Nikola was busy at work one afternoon when he heard a knock at the door. He decided to ignore it, as he did not like intrusions on his time. But the knocking became more insistent, and he angrily went to open the door. His annoyance soon changed to delight as he saw his friend George Westinghouse standing there. George wasn't smiling, though, and Nikola soon found out why.

George told Nikola that the Westinghouse company was in financial trouble. He said that the royalty checks that the company had been paying to Nikola had been draining the company of too much money. He was ready to declare bankruptcy and lose his company.

Nikola thought about how George had believed in him when no one else would listen. He told George that the benefits they had together given to the world with the AC system were worth more to him than money.

Nikola tore up his contract with the Westinghouse company, giving up his future royalties in order to save the company. This would mean the loss of several million dollars over Nikola's lifetime, but he saw only that he had helped out a friend and saved the company that would promote his AC system. He also made George promise that he would give the AC system to the world. Nikola trusted that his friend would keep his promise.

In tearing up the contract with the Westinghouse company, Nikola was depriving himself of funds needed for future research. But Nikola did not have a good business sense. His decision to accept no royalties for his patents seriously affected his future work. Now Nikola had to pick and choose which inventions he could work on, since he had only a limited supply of money for equipment.

After George Westinghouse left Nikola's lab that day, the inventor went back to his work as if nothing unusual had taken place. He had some money saved and he was still receiving a small amount from other patents that he had sold, so he was able to purchase more equipment and continue his work.

Nikola was more of a hermit now than ever before. He refused almost all invitations, with very few exceptions. But he knew it was important to continue to address certain scientific organizations and keep them aware of the work he was doing. So, in February 1893, when Nikola was invited to give a lecture at the Franklin Institute—a scientific and educational institute in Philadelphia—he accepted.

Standing in front of numerous scientists and electrical engineers, he boldly proposed a new theory. He said that the upper layers of the atmosphere—known as the ionosphere—were charged with electrical energy. If this charged layer could somehow be reached, he told his audience, it would be possible to send and receive sound waves through the atmosphere—perhaps even transmit voices. Some scientists shook their heads. Perhaps Tesla had gone a bit too far this time. But others were more receptive to what he was saying. Tesla was a genius. Perhaps it was possible. Then, a few months later, Nikola described the principles of wireless broadcasting to the National Electric Light Association in St. Louis, Missouri. Once again, Nikola made scientific history.

In St. Louis, Nikola gave a demonstration in which he sent a wireless message from a five-kilowatt transmitter to a receiver about 30 feet away. On a very small scale, this was the first public demonstration of wireless transmission—what would eventually be known as radio.

Although Nikola wished to remain as secluded as possible so that he could work undisturbed, a few close friends were always welcome in his lab. One of these friends was the writer Samuel Clemens, known as Mark Twain, author of *The Adventures of Huckleberry Finn*. Another welcome friend was George Westinghouse. Westinghouse never forgot that he had promised Nikola he would give alternating current to the world.

The opportunity finally came in 1893 when the World's Fair was about to open in Chicago, Illinois. The fair was named the Chicago World's Columbian Exposition to celebrate the 400th anniversary of Columbus's voyage to America. The fairgrounds covered more than 686 acres of lakefront property in Chicago and consisted of numerous small exhibition buildings.

Like many of Nikola's friends, Mark Twain (left) loved to watch the inventor at work. Below, Nikola creates the first portrait ever taken by phosphorescent light.

This fair was going to be spectacular. For the first time ever in the United States, an area as large as the World's Fair would be lit up with electric lights.

George Westinghouse had a contract to do all the lighting for the fair. The Westinghouse company would use the Tesla system: the engine, the dynamo, and the alternating-current generator.

Arrangements were made for President Grover Cleveland to turn on the lights from the White House in Washington, D.C. One of the most spectacular sights in the history of electricity occurred when, on opening day, the entire fairgrounds

The 1893 World's Fair in Chicago (above and opposite) *showed the world what Nikola's alternating-current system could do.*

sparkled with white light. People gasped in astonishment at this "White City." Then they applauded the two men who made it all possible—Nikola Tesla and George Westinghouse. For the first time, the public saw how alternating current could change their lives.

The World's Fair marked the end of the battle of the currents. Alternating current now became the acceptable and preferred method of generating electricity.

Thomas Edison's associates warned him that popular opinion sided with Nikola Tesla. But Edison was a stubborn man, and he refused to listen. He continued to design his engines and machines to work on direct current, acting as if alternating current did not exist.

Nikola had his own exhibition building at the fair. Here he demonstrated many of his new ideas and inventions. In one demonstration, Nikola showed a metal egg sitting on a small circular platform. The egg had no wires or strings attached to it. When Nikola threw a switch, the egg rotated on one end. People watched in wide-eyed wonder. In another demonstration, Nikola lit up wireless glass tubes that he held in his hands. The audience didn't know that Nikola was using energy generated by a Tesla coil in another room, so they saw the tubes light up as if by magic.

Finally, Nikola proved to the fair visitors that alternating current was not deadly, as Edison had tried to make them believe. For the first time outside the privacy of his lab, Nikola's body became a human target for millions of volts of electric

Nikola amazed audiences at the World's Fair with demonstrations such as holding this vacuum bulb, which seemed to light up by magic.

current generated by one of his coils. As always, he walked away unharmed.

People decided that Nikola must be a magician or a wizard. Some people went so far as to claim that he was from another planet. Nikola just laughed at their stories. He was simply using basic scientific principles. It was others' lack of understanding that made it seem like magic. He did not have any special powers.

After the excitement of the World's Fair began to subside, Nikola returned to his lab in New York. Coils, machines, and other paraphernalia cluttered the room. There were so many inventions that he had started but never finished because another new idea needed attention. Even now another new project loomed on the horizon.

People had been talking for a long time about using alternating current to light up their cities. Some farsighted engineers in upstate New York began to look at Niagara Falls in the same way Nikola had years before. They saw the falls as a source of power that nature had freely granted them. But how could they use that power to light the city of Buffalo, some 22 miles away? A call went out to engineers all over the country. Whoever could come up with a sensible and economical plan to harness the power of Niagara Falls would get the job and the fame.

Years earlier in Croatia, when Nikola had seen a picture of Niagara Falls, he had thought of harnessing its energy. In October 1893, Nikola's old friend George Westinghouse won the contract to harness the power of the falls. Using the Tesla system, he built three generators to light up the Niagara Falls area in 1895. The combined power of these generators was more than 14,000 horsepower. Nikola's dream was finally a reality!

Years after Nikola first saw a picture of Niagara Falls, George Westinghouse (above) harnessed the Falls' power by building generators that used the alternating-current system (below).

Now it was time to extend the power to the city of Buffalo. Westinghouse installed 11 more generators. Almost overnight, the power plant at Niagara Falls became the electrical wonder of the world. Nikola wrote: "I saw my ideas carried out at Niagara and I marveled at the mystery of the mind."

Westinghouse had proved not only that Nikola's discoveries could be put to practical use, but also that alternating current was one of the greatest discoveries of all time. Lord Kelvin, an English scientist, wrote: "Tesla has contributed more to electrical science than any man up to this time."

In November of 1893, Nikola was honored at the Franklin Institute with the prestigious Elliott Cresson medal, an award given by the American Institute of Electrical Engineers to scientists of great achievement. A few months later, a lavish dinner was given in New York to honor Nikola Tesla. Many people spoke about Nikola that night and publicly praised his work and his dedication. Nikola was asked to make a speech.

Nikola talked about this new "Age of Electricity." He spoke of his concern for the future energy needs of the planet:

> The time will come when the comfort, the very existence perhaps, of man will depend upon that wonderful agent [electricity].... Men will go to the waterfalls, to the tides.... There they will harness the energy and transmit the same to their settlements, to warm their homes by, to give them light, and to keep their obedient slaves, the machines, toiling.

Nikola in his laboratory with a Tesla coil

EIGHT

A New Science Is Born

1894–1898

Determined to make up for time he had spent developing the Niagara project, Nikola continued his work in 1894 with a feverish energy. He slept little, ate little, and worked like a madman. He developed more coils, larger and more powerful than the ones he had built before. He invented more advanced condensers and more powerful motors. He invented a system whereby he could light up the whole lab using wireless tubes. Finally, he began to do serious work in the field of resonance and vibrations.

A vibration is the rapid back-and-forth motion of an object, which creates waves in the air. Resonance is the effect of these waves on another object. For instance, if a violinist plays certain notes on a violin, the strings of the violin vibrate. The resonance of the vibrations can shatter a glass in the same room.

Nikola wanted to find out what effects resonance would have on metal and other substances. He built a machine called an oscillator that produced vibrations of varying frequencies. (All objects vibrate at a different frequency, depending on the density of their atoms.) Nikola wanted to test the oscillator. He ordered a two-foot-long piece of the finest quality steel. He attached the oscillator to the steel and fine-tuned it to the same frequency as the vibrations of the steel. It took a while, but as Nikola looked on, the steel began to vibrate faster and faster and finally broke.

Now he was even more intrigued. He wanted to learn more about this force. He knew he could not rest until he conducted more experiments.

The building that housed Nikola's laboratory had a steel framework that he thought would be perfect for his experiment. But what he didn't know was that this building's foundation rested on a sandbed that stretched for several blocks, as did all the other buildings in the area. While Nikola sat in his lab making adjustments to his oscillator, he was unaware

Nikola with one of his Tesla coils

that strange things were happening in his neighborhood. The sand beneath the buildings began to vibrate furiously, causing them to shake as if there was an earthquake.

At police headquarters two blocks away, windows blew out, sturdy brick walls shook, and the first floor of the building flooded due to a broken water pipe on the second floor. One of the police officers shouted that it was an earthquake. But another police officer suspected Nikola. Shaking the plaster off his hat, he stormed out of the building.

When the police arrived at Nikola's lab, they found one wall of the building partly demolished, and the front door off its hinges. Nikola was standing in a litter of fallen plaster, a sledge hammer in his hand. In front of him was the demolished oscillator.

With a grave expression, Nikola told the police officers that they were too late. The experiment was over.

Fortunately no one was hurt and no fires broke out from the ruptured gas pipes. The police could do nothing else but reprimand Nikola and go back to their station house to begin repairs.

Although his experiment had had a disastrous effect, Nikola did learn from it, and he was exhilarated by his success. He wanted to do further work in resonance, but after the problems caused by his oscillator, he realized that the heart of New York City was not the proper place. He needed to find another location, away from buildings and people. Until he found such a place, he would stop all experiments with resonance and work on other things.

Nikola's head was busy with new ideas, but there never seemed to be enough time or money to develop them all. His life's goal was to make the planet a better place for people to live. He wanted to make life easier and to enable people to use nature's gifts wisely. Therefore, he concentrated on developing the ideas that could have the most beneficial results for humankind.

Nikola Tesla should have been given credit in his lifetime as the inventor of the radio. He had patented his inventions and published his lectures. These lectures explained the basic requirements for successful wireless transmission—the same requirements used in every radio today. The whole electrical world knew of Nikola's success. But someone else received the credit—Guglielmo Marconi.

In 1895, Marconi gave a demonstration similar to the one Nikola Tesla had given two years before. Marconi proclaimed that his was the first public demonstration of wireless transmission, and that it was his own idea. Although Marconi strongly denied it, many people believed that he had read Nikola's printed lectures and used Nikola's designs. When Nikola heard about this, he merely said, "Let him continue. He is using 17 of my patents."

On March 13, 1895, at 2:30 A.M., Nikola was lying in bed thinking about his work, when he heard a knock at the door. Nikola opened it and found a police officer standing there. He told Nikola to come quickly. There had been a fire in Nikola's laboratory.

Nikola dressed as quickly as he could and followed the officer out of the hotel. As they arrived at his lab, Nikola could see smoke rising in the sky from the burning building. Firefighters were on the scene and had just gotten the flames under control. The fire chief told Nikola that they weren't able to save anything. As his men were about to enter the

Guglielmo Marconi received credit for one of Nikola's most important inventions—radio.

building, the second floor had caved in. Tons of equipment crashed to the ground. Fortunately, no one was injured.

Nikola listened to the fire chief without saying a word. He could feel hot tears stinging his eyes. He took a deep breath and tried to be strong. All his notes, books, and electrical equipment were destroyed. He was about to make his first long-distance demonstration of the wireless and all his research was now gone. As one newspaper reported it: "His work of a lifetime was swept away."

Nikola had very little money left. Most of the money that he had received from his patents had been invested in the equipment that was now totally destroyed. He wondered if there was anyone who had enough money to finance him and help him rebuild his lab.

Fortunately, Nikola didn't have to wonder for long. News of the fire had spread all around the city, and it reached the ears of Edward Dean Adams, a man who had worked on the Niagara Falls project. He was very upset when he thought that all of Nikola's work had been destroyed. He admired Nikola and felt that it would be a terrible injustice if this great inventor couldn't go on with his experiments. Adams offered Nikola $100,000 to rebuild his lab and purchase new equipment. Four months later, in July of 1895, 39-year-old Nikola opened a new lab on Houston Street in New York City.

Once Nikola was settled in his new lab, he continued his work on radio transmission. He conducted many experiments, trying to build more powerful transmitters and receivers. In the early part of 1897, Nikola filed a patent for his basic radio design (although it wasn't granted until 1900). Then he had another idea. If energy could be transmitted over a distance, then it must also be possible to control mechanical devices from a distance. This started Nikola on a new but related area of research—the science of robotics.

The word *robotics* was not in use until 1917. Nikola used the word *teleautomatics* to describe this science. (The word *teleautomatics* comes from the Greek word *tele,* which means "from a distance," and *automatica,* which means "self-moving.")

In September 1898, Nikola announced plans to build a radio remote-controlled boat. He told people that his boat would not have any wires attached to it, nor an engine inside it. Its movements would be controlled from a distance. Many people laughed at Nikola's idea. Tesla will look like a fool, they said to one another.

Doubt turned to awe when Nikola gave a demonstration in Madison Square Garden in New York City. As always when appearing in front of a large audience, Nikola was impeccably dressed. He wore a black suit with tails, a white tie, and a top hat. There was still a great deal of the entertainer in this inventor. He enjoyed performing in front of large audiences, astounding them with things they had never seen before.

Nikola stood a few feet away from a huge metal tank in the center of the auditorium. He had constructed a 13-foot-long metal boat, which sat in the middle of the tank awaiting Nikola's commands. He began by giving the boat commands that made it move around the tank and then dive under the water. Then he asked the audience to call out commands to

Nikola used this remote-controlled boat to demonstrate his work in the field of teleautomatics.

the boat. Standing on the other side of the room, operating the remote-control device, Nikola moved the boat according to the commands. The audience was speechless. The impossible had become real right in front of their eyes. This boat was Nikola's first invention in the science of robotics.

Nikola also designed plans for guided missiles long before they were ever thought possible. In 1898, Nikola filed the first patent for radio remote control in guided missiles.

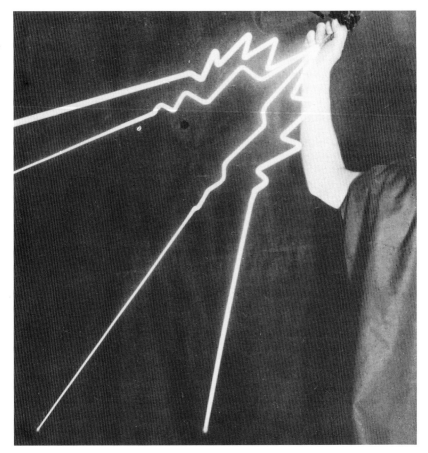

Experiments in Nikola's lab were often dramatic.

It was difficult for Nikola to work on all of his ideas. There just wasn't enough time and the world was still too technologically immature for many of his plans. His inventions in the field of teleautomatics planted the seeds for something different and exciting, but he felt that more important technological advances were possible in the field of energy transmission. Nikola told a *New York Times* reporter: "We are whirling through endless space with an inconceivable speed, all around us everything is spinning, everything is moving, everywhere is energy. There must be some way of availing ourselves of this energy more directly."

The same year that Nikola made his discoveries in the field of teleautomatics, he discovered a way to use the rays of the sun. He designed a machine to harness what is now known as solar energy. His machine could use the sun's rays to create steam, and, using a chemical solution, maintain the temperature of the steam during cloudy days and nightfall. Nikola saw great potential for solar energy, and he wanted to perfect his design so that he could present the gift of "free" energy to the world.

It was this principle that colored all of his work. Nikola firmly believed that energy was contained in and around the planet and throughout the whole universe. If people could be taught to harness these energy sources, they would not have to pay electric companies high prices to light and heat their homes.

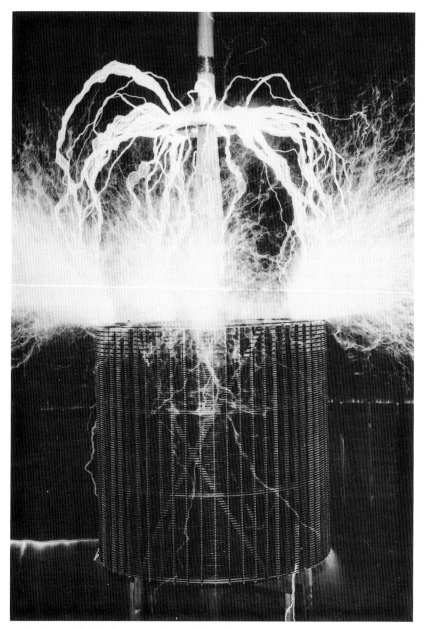

Nikola built his largest Tesla coil at his Colorado Springs laboratory.

NINE

Colorado Springs

1899–1900

One day in 1899, Nikola received a letter from a Mr. Curtis, a patent attorney for the Westinghouse Corporation. George Westinghouse had mentioned to Mr. Curtis that his friend Nikola Tesla felt stifled in his research because of his location in the middle of New York City.

Mr. Curtis was a great admirer of Nikola. He thought Mr. Tesla should have a laboratory far from the city and away from the intruding public. Mr. Curtis had done a good deal of work for the Colorado Springs Electric Company, and he thought that Nikola might want to set up a lab there. Nikola would be in the mountains, surrounded by miles of unpopulated land. Here he could conduct major experiments without fear of endangering people or their property. Mr. Curtis sent a letter to Nikola telling him about this plan.

Nikola quickly responded, thanking Mr. Curtis for his help and expressing his needs:

> My coils are producing 4,000,000 volts. Sparks jumping from walls to ceilings are a fire hazard. I must have electrical power, water, and my own laboratory. I will need a good carpenter who will follow instructions. I

am being financed for this by Astor, Crawford, and Simpson [wealthy men in New York City who offered to give Nikola money for his research]. My work will be done late at night when the power load will be least.

Mr. Curtis made all the arrangements for Nikola. He chose the site that he felt would be most conducive to Nikola's experiments. He arranged for land to be loaned to Nikola at no cost. All the electricity for the lab would be free as well. Nikola was excited. He knew that this would be a major leap forward for his work. He packed up the equipment and papers from his New York laboratory and arranged to have them shipped to Colorado Springs. He bought tickets for the next train to Colorado.

Nikola's goals in Colorado Springs were quite ambitious. He wanted to develop a worldwide communication system, and he intended to send a wireless message from Colorado Springs to Paris. He also wanted to learn how to send free energy to any place on the globe.

For weeks he watched the local carpenter and his assistant hammer away at the wooden beams that would eventually be the frame for his laboratory and home. It was an enormous structure, with a roof that opened and a huge, 70-foot-tall tower. In the rear of the building stood a 200-foot pole with a copper ball about 3 feet in diameter attached to the top of it. This pole would be the key to his long-distance energy transmission.

The lab was surrounded by a fence that displayed warning signs to local residents: "WARNING, DANGER! DO NOT ENTER!" Nikola didn't have the time or the patience to deal with curious neighbors while he was working.

Nikola worked day and night in his lab, taking very little time for recreation. His enjoyment came from his work. Sometimes he would take long walks in the countryside that surrounded his lab, thinking about an experiment that was under way, or about one that he wanted to begin.

One night he witnessed an unusual storm in the area. Lightning created a spectacle of extreme brilliance in the sky. But this was not ordinary lightning. The bolts were formed in arcs instead of straight lines. This phenomenon is known as arc lightning.

Nikola found this natural occurrence important, because he realized that he was observing what are commonly referred to as "stationary waves." These are waves of electrical energy surrounding the earth and frozen in position. Nikola knew that the power transmission he had dreamed of could be achieved quite easily by using this energy. He had made a great discovery.

"The earth is alive with electrical vibrations," he wrote in his journal that day.

Nikola began to see many uses for this energy, including sending wireless telegraphic messages over long distances. He also thought that it would be possible to transmit the human voice over any distance on the earth without losing the quality of the sound.

Nikola didn't know exactly how long his money would hold out, but he knew that with the enormous amounts he was spending on equipment and materials, his funds would quickly be gone. He also suspected that his financial backers were fickle. The next time he asked for money, they might not be in the mood to help him. Therefore, Nikola prized his time in Colorado Springs, knowing that at any time he might have to return to New York.

One of the first things Nikola did after building his lab was to build a giant coil, the largest Tesla coil ever constructed.

Exterior (right) *and interior*
(opposite) *views of Nikola's*
Colorado Springs laboratory

It was a 12-million-volt machine that created sparks up to 135 feet long. Nikola had discovered that there was a vast supply of electricity at the core of the earth. He had the idea that if he supercharged it with his giant coil from Colorado, it would provide electricity all over the planet. People on land or at sea could use all the electricity they wanted just by transmitting it from the ground—all free of charge.

When news of what Nikola was doing got back to New York, his financial backers became very upset. How dare Nikola make free electricity available to the public! Didn't he know that he could put all the major electrical companies out of business? Nikola's funds were cut off. There would be no more money for research.

The inventor took the news quite calmly. He had expected as much. These men cared only about making money. Now his dreams of sending wireless messages across the Atlantic and providing the public with free energy would probably not be realized. He still had some money left, however, and money meant time and materials. Nikola telegraphed his assistants at the lab in New York to send him more equipment as fast as possible.

One of his final experiments before leaving Colorado was to create artificial lightning. Nikola believed that if he could duplicate the forces of nature that created lightning, he would be that much closer to understanding how to harness these forces for other uses.

Nikola was confident that his experiment would be a success. The giant coil in the center of the room and the 200-foot mast on top of the lab would be the vital keys to this experiment, but it was extremely dangerous. Nikola's assistant in Colorado Springs, Kolman Czito, had been working for Nikola for years. He knew they would be taking a very big chance. There was a strong possibility that they could get killed by their own lightning bolts or that the lab could be burned to the ground. But he was very loyal to the inventor.

Standing in the doorway of the lab, Nikola gave Czito the signal to throw the switch. They both held their breath. What they saw soon gave them reason to smile. It was an amazing spectacle. Streaks of artificial lightning swirled in the sky around the mast, high above the lab. Lightning continued to explode over and over again, hurling bolts into the air for more than 100 feet above the mast. Inside the lab, a soft blue light filled the room. Threadlike lines of flame and electrical sparks shot out in all directions from the coils on the transformer.

Nikola was awed by his success. Never before had he felt so in tune with the natural forces of the earth or so confident that all people would eventually harness these forces and use them for the good of the planet. He watched the electrical display, deep in thought, when suddenly everything stopped abruptly. The lab was thrown into darkness.

Nikola had used so much electrical power for his coils that he had knocked out the generator at the Colorado Springs power station and set it on fire. The entire town was without power.

The Colorado Springs Electric Company was not pleased that Mr. Tesla had caused them so much trouble. They refused to supply any more electrical power to his lab. Nikola pleaded with them to reconsider their decision. Without electricity, his work would be finished. He made a deal with the company. He would repair their generator at his own expense if they would give him power again. They agreed to his plan and Nikola was back at work within a week.

On one of Nikola's last evenings in Colorado Springs, he was absorbed in making adjustments to a radio receiver. He knew that he wouldn't rest that night until it was done. Suddenly he noticed that sounds were coming from the receiver in a regular pattern from outside the earth's atmosphere.

Nikola paced the room in excitement. There could be only one explanation, he thought. Some being on another planet was trying to signal Earth! His excitement grew as he convinced himself that he was indeed picking up "messages" from the universe.

In a way, Nikola was correct, although the transmissions were not being produced by any planetary beings. Astronomers now know that the stars give off radio waves in a regular pattern. Nikola detected these waves at least 20 years before astronomers did. Had he known where they were coming from, he might have been deeply moved that he had been one of the first to receive a message from the stars.

Nikola in his Long Island, New York, laboratory

TEN

The Final Project: Radio City

1901–1917

When Nikola returned to New York after closing up his lab in Colorado Springs, he had very little money left. His meager savings were almost gone, and he had just enough to live on. His financial backers had forsaken him, and he was once again thrown back on his own. But Nikola still had a dream. He wanted to build a city entirely devoted to long-distance communications around the globe.

Nikola was a very proud man who had difficulty asking for help. But his dreams were more important to him than pride. Once again, he appealed to some of the wealthy New Yorkers that he knew for financial support.

One of the people to whom his plea was directed was a wealthy financier named J. P. Morgan. Morgan had built one of the largest financial empires of the century, and he had more than enough money to give to Nikola. He knew of Nikola's reputation as a great inventor, but he wanted proof that a loan to Nikola would earn a substantial profit. J. P. Morgan never invested his money unless he was assured that his investment would yield a large return.

Nikola was invited to Mr. Morgan's home. He tried to share his ideas with the great financier. Nikola explained his idea of building a "world city"—a center for world communication. He told Mr. Morgan that at the heart of the city would

Financier J. P. Morgan invested in Nikola's final project.

be a huge transmitter, capable of sending wireless messages around the world. People could talk to each other around the globe through a small instrument no larger than one's hand. Distance would be no problem.

And there was more. The specifics of Nikola's plan included the free distribution of energy to needy parts of the world. Nikola also wanted to create and produce various remote-control household appliances so that people could be free from housework and devote more time to the activities they enjoyed.

Mr. Morgan was unimpressed. He knew about Nikola Tesla. He knew that while Nikola was a genius in the field of electrical engineering, he was also a man who had many grandiose ideas—ideas that cost a lot of money to put into operation but had very little monetary return.

Nikola tried another approach. This time he had something to offer Mr. Morgan. He proposed to sell the financier 51 percent of the patent rights to his inventions for $150,000. Nikola knew that $150,000 was not enough money to complete his project, but he hoped that once under way, the project would be financed by other investors interested in his enterprise. This was a proposal that Mr. Morgan liked.

With $150,000 to begin construction of his city, Nikola looked for a place to begin building. A land developer on Long Island (about sixty miles outside of New York City) offered to sell a 2,000-acre tract of land to the inventor.

The construction of the city of Wardenclyffe, as Nikola named it, had begun. The lab would be housed in a huge brick building. Nikola was anxious for it to be completed, since he needed a lot of space to house his machines and materials from both the New York City lab and the lab in Colorado Springs.

The second order of business was to construct a 154-foot tower made of wooden beams and topped by a huge spherical copper dome. Nikola had made very precise mathematical calculations based on the height of the tower. He concluded that a spherical dome with a diameter of 100 feet would be the most efficient way to transmit and receive radio waves. Before construction of the tower was ever completed, however, Nikola ran into a couple of problems. First of all, he ran out of money. Once again he asked J. P. Morgan for money. This time Morgan loaned it to Nikola with surprisingly little hesitation. By now Mr. Morgan was convinced that Nikola could achieve success with his project and that he, Morgan, would become famous as the man who made the building of the great Radio City possible.

Nikola's second problem was a constant struggle—getting his materials on time. Motors and dynamos were not easily

Nikola planned to broadcast information all over the world with this tower, but it never became operational.

produced because of their unusual design. Equipment for their manufacture had to be specially ordered, a process that caused unwanted delays. Without these materials, however, Nikola could not complete the final step of his plan—to set up a world broadcasting station.

Nikola decided to publish a pamphlet advertising his project. He called it the World System and described its goal of worldwide wireless communication. He wrote:

> By its means, for instance, a telephone subscriber here may call up any other subscriber on the globe. An inexpensive receiver, not bigger than a watch, will enable him to listen anywhere on land or sea, to a speech delivered or music played in some other place, however distant.

Nikola planned to have the station ready for operation within nine months. In his brochure, he listed the things that would be possible with his World System. Some of these were:

> The establishment of a secret government telegraph service...the universal distribution of general news...the establishment of a marine service enabling navigators of all ships to steer perfectly without a compass to prevent collisions and disasters...the reproduction anywhere in the world of photographic pictures and all kinds of drawings or records.

The interior of Nikola's Long Island laboratory

It seemed as though all of Nikola's life work would culminate in this final project—all of his inventions and ideas would be used to create a magnificent communications network. Sadly, the entire Wardenclyffe project failed.

Lack of finances once again caused Nikola anguish. Mr. Morgan was now losing interest in the project. He had invested a great deal of his money and almost a year had passed without as much as a dollar in return.

Mr. Morgan was not the only person who thought that Nikola's project at Wardenclyffe was a waste of time. Others who helped finance Nikola's projects over the years now wanted to collect the money due them. They thought Nikola was wasting his time on a foolish idea. They wanted him to put his energy into something that could make money so that he could pay them back. Nikola was broke. Where would he get all of this money from?

The only way to raise money was to sell his lab in Colorado Springs. Nikola did so immediately. Most of the money was given to his creditors. In 1902, less than two years after Nikola began construction on his city, he knew that his dream would soon be coming to an end. No one believed in him anymore, and there was no money to support his work.

If Nikola had had a better business sense, he might have had enough money to see him through a lifetime of projects. Not only did Nikola give away more than a million dollars when he tore up his contract with Westinghouse, he also refused to take the time to pursue other companies that used his patents without paying him royalties.

Before he closed the door on his lab at Wardenclyffe for the last time, however, the inventor decided to give the local residents something to remember him by. On the night of July 15, 1903, Nikola sent lightning from the dome streaking across the sky hundreds of miles in all directions. The *New York Sun,* a local newspaper, reported:

> Tesla's flashes are startling, but he won't tell us what it is he is trying to do at Wardenclyffe. Natives hereabouts are intensely interested in the electrical display shown from the tall tower where Nikola Tesla is conducting his experiments in wireless...all sorts of lightning flashed from the tall tower and poles last night. For a time, the air around was filled with glittering electricity which seemed to shoot off into the darkness on some mysterious errand.

After leaving Wardenclyffe, Nikola returned to his lab in New York. He was greatly disappointed that his dream had ended before he had a chance to show the world the potential of his communications system. But Nikola had other projects to work on. He wanted to focus on improving his alternating-current system and developing a miniature turbine.

Years before, Nikola had built his largest turbine, which was being used at Niagara Falls. Now he was designing and building a bladeless turbine no longer than a human hand. The mini-turbine was six inches long, weighed about ten pounds, and used a 200-horsepower engine. Nikola called it a "powerhouse in a hat."

The mini-turbine's appeal was in its mechanical simplicity. It needed little adjustment to work at full potential. It was also inexpensive to construct and needed only a competent mechanic to replace its parts. It would last almost indefinitely.

In 1906 Nikola was again badly in need of financial support. He was receiving money for his early patents, but this wasn't enough to allow him to continue with his work. When he failed to interest some manufacturers in investing money

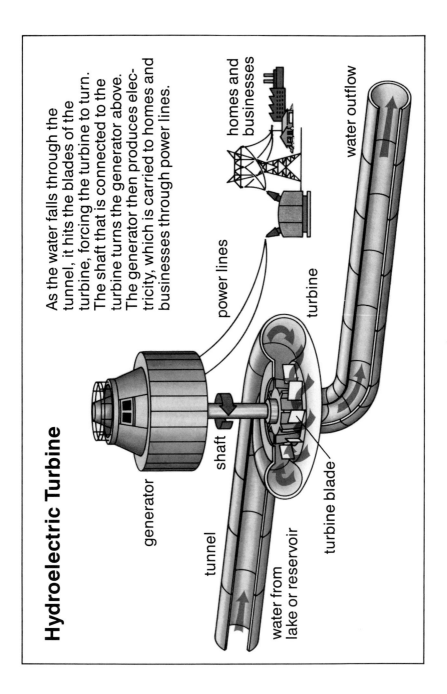

Hydroelectric Turbine

As the water falls through the tunnel, it hits the blades of the turbine, forcing the turbine to turn. The shaft that is connected to the turbine turns the generator above. The generator then produces electricity, which is carried to homes and businesses through power lines.

homes and businesses

power lines

water outflow

turbine

generator

shaft

tunnel

water from lake or reservoir

turbine blade

in his turbine, he went back to his lab determined to work with the little money he had left. For years he had been on a roller coaster ride with fame and fortune. He was a millionaire before he was 40 years old, but by the time he reached 50 he had very little money left. Nikola was becoming discouraged with the way the world was reacting to his work.

Then, in 1915, at the age of 59, Nikola was told that he, along with Thomas Edison, would be awarded the Nobel Prize in physics for their work in electricity. This prestigious award is given every year to the scientist or scientists who have made the most outstanding contribution in their particular field of study.

When news came from Europe that both Tesla and Edison were to share in the prize, reporters made appointments to interview both men. Neither Nikola nor Edison had been notified yet and they both expressed surprise at the news.

Unfortunately, disappointment was in store for both of them. A few days later, official announcements were made that the Nobel Prize for physics would go to two British scientists for their research in the structure of crystals.

Americans were disappointed. It would have been an honor to have two American scientists accept the award. Nikola took the news calmly. Although the Nobel Prize was the highest recognition and honor in the world—and included a monetary prize of $20,000—Nikola was not sure he had wanted to accept it. Thomas Edison would have been a co-recipient of the award. Nikola felt that Edison had hampered, rather than helped, the development of electricity with his ruthless campaign against alternating current. Nikola did not think that Edison deserved the award.

Two years later, in 1917, the American Institute of Electrical Engineers (AIEE) announced that Nikola Tesla was to be awarded the Edison Medal. This award was given each year in Edison's name for recognition of major contributions to the field of electricity.

But Nikola did not want the award. He felt that the AIEE had taken too long to publicly recognize him and his work. They had ignored the man who was responsible for more advances in the field of electricity than they had witnessed in many years.

B. A. Behrend, one of the scientists who had been instrumental in nominating Tesla, visited the inventor in his office several times, trying to persuade him to accept the award.

Nikola (front row, right) *attended a dinner honoring civic leader Henry Clews.*

But Nikola told him: "It is nearly 30 years since I announced my rotating magnetic field and the alternating-current system before the Institute. I do not need its honors and someone else may find it useful."

Nikola went on to express other bitter feelings. He told Behrend:

> You propose to honor me with a medal which I could pin on my coat...you would decorate my body and continue to let starve my mind and its creative products which have supplied the foundation upon which the major portion of your Institute exists.

But Behrend would not give up. After persistently continuing to show up at Nikola's office, he was finally able to persuade Nikola to accept the award. At an elaborate dinner given in Nikola's honor in New York City, the inventor accepted the award to the loud applause of the members of the Institute. Mr. Behrend gave an eloquent speech:

> Were we to seize and eliminate from our industrial world the results of Mr. Tesla's work, the wheels of industry would cease to turn, our electric cars [trolleys] and trains would stop, our towns would be dark, our mills would be dead and idle. So far-reaching is his work, it has become the warp and woof of industry.

ELEVEN

A Final Tribute

1918–1943

In 1918, 62-year-old Nikola Tesla was still a distinguished-looking gentleman. He was always well dressed, although many of his clothes were old-fashioned and outdated. Outdoors, he was always seen with white gloves in one hand and a cane in the other. He didn't wear any rings or other ornaments. Although he was no longer young, Nikola walked tall and straight, with the air of someone important.

Nikola was living in a small room in a New York City hotel and working out of a small office in another building. Each morning he would go to the office, where he would open his mail, answer letters, prepare his lectures, and draw designs for new devices that he wished to patent. But most of his work was still done in his head. Throughout his life, he had maintained the uncanny ability to design, build, and test an invention before putting it on paper or building it.

World War I had been raging for three years and people around the country could think and talk of little else. Because of the war's damaging effect on industry, Nikola was unable to manufacture two very practical inventions at the time, an automobile speedometer and a motor for small aircraft. Nikola tried to sell the plans for the speedometer to a company in Chicago, but the automotive industry, which was relatively new, had come to a halt when the United States entered the

Nikola spent the final years of his life living in this hotel.

war. Nikola then tried to interest the National Committee on Aeronautics in his motor. This motor had an important advantage over other small-craft motors because it weighed considerably less. Unfortunately, the government wasn't interested. There was a war on. No one had time to look at Nikola's new designs.

Nikola continued to work on any new ideas that he thought might help humanity. He got into the habit of holding a press conference every year on his birthday. He invited reporters from local magazines and newspapers to dinner, where he would tell them about the new inventions he was working on. One of his favorite themes was ecological balance on the planet.

He often voiced warnings that the planet needed to be cared for. Nikola told everyone that the earth held many secrets, which it would gladly reveal, if people only took the time to ask.

Sometimes at these birthday celebrations Nikola made predictions about the future. In a birthday interview in January 1926, when Nikola was 70 years old, a reporter asked the inventor to talk about what he thought the next 70 years would bring. Nikola told the reporter:

> Before the end of this century, you will be able to communicate instantly by simple vest pocket equipment. We shall be able to witness and hear events: the inauguration of a President, the playing of a World Series game, the havoc of an earthquake, or the terror of a battle—just as though we were present. Aircraft will travel the skies, unmanned, driven and guided by radio. Enormous power will be transmitted great distances without wires. Earthquakes will become more and more frequent. Temperate zones will turn frigid or torrid...and some of these awe-inspiring developments are not so far off.

In 1926 Nikola experienced a deep sorrow when his friend Katharine Johnson died. She had been ill for some time. During her illness, Katharine wrote many letters to Nikola in which she shared many intimate feelings with him. She especially told him of her feelings of frustration. Katharine felt that had she been a man, she could have lived a more fulfilling life, perhaps with her own career and more independence. But she felt she had been held back from many of life's opportunities because she was a woman. She envied Nikola's exciting career as a scientist.

As the years went on, Nikola became more reclusive. He had always been eccentric. He was very specific about the kinds of food that he would eat. Now, in his later years, his meals often consisted of a bowl of warm milk. His eating habits remained odd. Obsessed by numbers that were divisible by three, he always required eighteen cloth napkins to be placed near his plate so that he could clean each glass, utensil, and dish before using them and then discard the napkin. Also, whenever he needed to wipe his mouth during the meal, he used a clean napkin. This eccentricity also applied to the number of towels that he required in the bathroom. He insisted that either fifteen or eighteen clean towels be on hand when he washed or bathed.

Nikola's passion for his work made him seem odd and antisocial to many people. Yet when new friendships found him, he was open to them. One new friend was a young Yugoslavian sculptor, Ivan Mestrovic. Ivan was famous in his native country. He was visiting the United States with the intention of making the American people aware of his work.

Perhaps because of their common heritage, Ivan and Nikola became good friends. They took long walks and talked about many things: politics, science, current events, and poetry. They both loved the Serbian poets, and they often discussed poems and recited lines they remembered.

After Ivan returned to Yugoslavia, he received a letter from Nikola commissioning him to sculpt a bust of the inventor. Nikola wrote that he wasn't able to pay for it all at once, but would Ivan consider taking small payments? Ivan was honored that Nikola would think enough of his work to commission him. He wrote back that he would do a bust of Nikola for nothing.

In 1931 some of Nikola's old friends and acquaintances gave a party for his 75th birthday. Telegrams poured in from all over the world. They were from scientists in all fields of work who wanted to express their immense gratitude to Nikola Tesla for his achievements. They said that Nikola had been an inspiration to them in their own endeavors. Some of the telegrams read:

> To men like yourself who have learned firsthand the secrets of nature and who have shown us how her laws may be applied...we owe a debt that cannot be paid.

> There is no doubt that the name of Tesla is as great as the name of Faraday is in the discovery of the phenomenon underlying all electrical work.

> If one reads your works today—at a time when radio has attained such a world significance—one is astonished at how many of your suggestions, often under another's name, have later been realized.

Nikola also published papers that year on two important designs: a plan for generating electricity from seaweed, and a design for a steam plant that would run on geothermal energy, or heat from inside the earth. He even designed a ship that could run on geothermal energy. But once again, lack of funds was an obstacle. No one was willing to invest in Nikola's ideas anymore.

Nikola's financial difficulties got worse as he got older. The Yugoslavian government gave him a small stipend of $7,200 a year, on which he could live comfortably, but his royalty checks had stopped. Most of the inventor's patents had expired, and they were now in the public domain—anyone had the right to use Nikola's designs without paying royalties. Without money from his designs, he had no source of income other than his government allowance. Occasionally, the hotel where he was living would threaten to make him move because he couldn't pay his bill. When this happened, old friends would come by and help him out with some extra money.

Nikola (second from left) *greets King Peter of Yugoslavia* (second from right) *in 1942.*

Nikola did not let his financial difficulties get him down, however. He was optimistic about himself and about the future of the world. One of the things that made people like him was that he spoke of the value of his inventions to the world, not of the greatness of his own work. He wrote:

> ...I continually experience an inexpressible satisfaction from the knowledge that my polyphase system [alternating-current system] is used throughout the world to lighten the burden of mankind and increase comfort and happiness and that my wireless system...is employed to render a service to and bring pleasure to people in all parts of the earth.

In 1936 Nikola was 80 years old. He led a very secluded life. He spent his days in his hotel, meditating and thinking. His head was still bursting with new ideas, but he knew that his physical strength would not last much longer. The maids in the hotel would look in on him from time to time. They were very fond of the eccentric Nikola.

But Nikola had a secret. Every night around midnight, he would go for a walk in his neighborhood. He never left for his walk without a bag of birdseed in his hand. His favorite place was in front of the New York Public Library. Here, pigeons by the hundreds would flock to the sidewalk waiting for seed from their friend. No one knew about his nocturnal excursions. It

In the last years of his life, Nikola loved to feed pigeons in front of the New York Public Library.

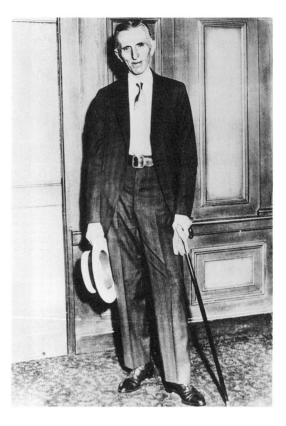

Nikola in front of his rooms at the Hotel New Yorker

would have been hard for anyone to believe that this tall, well-dressed man feeding the pigeons was the famous Nikola Tesla.

Nikola didn't have to go for a walk in order to feed the birds. Sometimes, he would just whistle to them from his window. Flocks of birds would fly to the ledge, some of them entering Nikola's bedroom, alighting on his bed and desk. Here, he talked to them and shared whatever seed he had among them. He never missed a day feeding his friends. It was as if he knew that they depended on him and he wouldn't let them down.

One of the pigeons that Nikola paid special attention to over the years was a beautiful, pure white bird with light gray tips on its wings. She seemed to have a special fondness for the inventor. Nikola was so familiar with this bird that he later claimed that he could pick her out of a flock of a thousand.

"No matter where I was that pigeon would find me," he told a friend. "When I wanted her I had only to wish and call her and she would come flying to me. She understood me and I understood her. I loved that pigeon and she loved me."

One day, Nikola noticed that the pigeon was ill. He stayed home from his lab for three days, nursing it back to health. As his ability to work diminished, the pigeon became his sole purpose for living. Then one day she flew into Nikola's window with a message.

> As I looked at her I knew she wanted to tell me she was dying. And then, as I got her message, there came the light from her eyes—powerful beams of light. Yes, it was a real light, a powerful, dazzling blinding light, a light more intense than I had ever produced by the most powerful lamps in my laboratory.

The death of that pigeon deeply affected Nikola. He was saddened and more lonely than he had ever been in his life. He felt that his life's work was finished.

Nikola died in his hotel room on January 7, 1943. He was 86 years old. The doctors listed the cause of death as heart failure due to old age.

Thousands of people crowded the Cathedral of St. John the Divine in New York City to honor Nikola Tesla at his funeral. Although the country was in the middle of World War II, hundreds of people from all over the world found time to send telegrams of tribute to this great electrical scientist. They honored a man who was "without a shade of doubt...the world's greatest inventor, not only at present but in all history.... His discoveries have no equal in the annals of the intellectual world."

This bust of Nikola, sculpted by his good friend Ivan Mestrovic, sits in the Tesla Museum in Belgrade, Serbia.

Epilogue

Every year, on January 7, the anniversary of Nikola Tesla's death, an elderly man patiently stands on the steps in front of the Tesla Museum in Belgrade, Yugoslavia, waiting for the museum to open. The gentleman is dressed in a black tailored suit, much like the one Nikola wore almost all his life, and in the gentleman's hand rests a red carnation.

When the door opens, the mysterious man talks to no one. He makes his way quietly to one particular room in the museum. Here, in the center of the room, sitting on a pedestal, is a golden globe containing the ashes of Nikola Tesla. The visitor stops before the globe and remains respectfully silent for a few moments, then places the red carnation on the pedestal, bows, and leaves the room.

This man moves on to the hall where the bust of Tesla sculpted by his friend Ivan Mestrovic stands. A statement by the great inventor is engraved beneath it. The words begin:

> The progressive development of man is virtually dependent on invention. It is the most important product of his creative brain. Its ultimate purpose is the complete mastery of mind over the material world, the harnessing of the forces of nature to human needs. This is the difficult task of the inventor who is often misunderstood and unrewarded....

The Tesla Museum houses Nikola's funeral urn and a mask made of Nikola after his death.

After silently reading the message, the visitor proclaims aloud, "This was a man!"

Nikola gained an enormous recognition and respect during certain periods of his life, and the honors continue to the present day.

In 1956, 100 years after Nikola's birth, celebrations took place in both Europe and the United States. In the United States, scholarships were awarded in his honor, a school in Chicago was named after him, and museums across the country organized special exhibits commemorating Tesla's extraordinary gifts to modern technology. In Munich, Germany, the International Electrotechnical Commission named an international scientific unit after the great inventor, called the "tesla." The tesla is a unit used in measuring magnetic fields.

In 1975 the Institute of Electrical Engineers established the Nikola Tesla award. This award is given each year to the individual who has made the most outstanding contribution to the field of electricity.

In addition to the Tesla Museum, Nikola was honored with a stamp bearing his image and a picture of the AC induction motor.

On the Electrical Building in Strasbourg, France, Nikola's name has a permanent place with other innovators in the field of electricity. In New York City, a street is named for the inventor.

In the fall of 1975, the Tesla Memorial Society was created. This organization consists of scientists, professional people, and citizens who wish to keep Nikola Tesla's name alive. The organization tries to make the country aware of his great achievements.

Nikola would have been pleased to know that in 1980, plans were finalized for the construction of several geothermal plants around the globe. In these plants, scientists are further developing the research that Nikola started almost 50 years before.

In 1983 the governor of Pennsylvania declared Nikola Tesla Day to honor his achievements. On September 21 of that year, the U.S. Postal Service paid tribute to Nikola Tesla by issuing a commemorative stamp in his honor.

In 1984 the state of Colorado issued an official proclamation. The governor of the state declared Nikola Tesla Month to mark the 100th anniversary of Nikola's arrival in the United States. The month was filled with several informative and interesting events to honor the work of this inventor.

In July of 1989, the governor of Pennsylvania again declared Nikola Tesla Day, urging all citizens to recognize the contributions of this great inventor and scientist.

The Tesla Museum in Belgrade holds all of Nikola's papers, diaries, and designs that were found in his hotel room after his death. Also in the museum are Nikola's remote-controlled boat, his coils, and several of his other inventions.

Nikola Tesla's life is perhaps best summed up in the words of Nikola's fellow scientist, B. A. Behrend, who paraphrased these famous lines from a poem by Alexander Pope:

> Nature and Nature's laws lay hid in night:
> God said, Let Tesla be, and all was light.

Sources

All quotes are taken from *My Inventions* by Nikola Tesla (Hart Brothers, 1982) except for the following:

p.93   V. Popovic, M. Bulajic, J. Nikolajevic, M. Karanovic, eds., *Nikola Tesla: Life and Work of a Genius.* (Belgrade: Nikola Tesla Museum, 1976), 38.

p.105   Margaret Cheney, *Tesla: Man Out of Time,* (Prentice-Hall, Inc., 1977), 163.

p.116   John J. O'Neill, *Prodigal Genius,* (Angriff Press, 1944), 209.

p.117   Ibid., 210-211.

p.119   Cheney, *Man Out of Time,* 163.

p.123   O'Neill, *Prodigal Genius,* 231.

p.123   Ibid., 236.

p.127   *Collier's Weekly,* January 30, 1926, interview with Nikola Tesla by John B. Kennedy.

p.129   Cheney, *Man Out of Time,* 238.

p.130   O'Neill, *Prodigal Genius,* 274-275.

p.133   *Tesla Journal,* v. 6 & 7, "Tesla's Point of View," 39.

p.139   Cheney, *Man Out of Time,* 217.

Bibliography

Books

Auto, P. *Yugoslavia.* New York: Walker & Co., 1965.

Cheney, Margaret. *Tesla: Man Out of Time.* Prentice-Hall, Inc., 1977

Davidson, Marshall B. *New York.* New York: Charles Scribner's Sons, 1977.

Halpern, J. *A Serbian Village.* New York: Harper & Row, 1967.

Knight, David C. *Robots: Past, Present, and Future.* New York: Wm. Morrow & Co., 1983.

Litterick, Ian. *Robots and Intelligent Machines.* New York: The Bookwright Press, 1984.

Nyrop, Richard F., ed. *Yugoslavia: A Country Study.* Washington, D.C.: The American University, 1982.

O'Neill, John J. *Prodigal Genius.* Angriff Press, 1944.

Popovic, Vojin, ed. *Tribute to Nikola Tesla.* Belgrade: Nikola Tesla Museum, 1961.

Popovic, Vojin, Radoslav Horvat, Nikola Nikolic, eds., *Nikola Tesla: Lectures Patents, Articles.* Belgrade: Nikola Tesla Museum, 1961.

Rutland, Jonathan. *Exploring the World of Robots.* New York: Warwick Press, 1979.

Still, Bayard. *Mirror for Gotham*. New York: University Press, 1956.
Tesla, Nikola. *Colorado Springs Notes*. Belgrade: Nikola Tesla Museum, 1978.
Tesla, Nikola. *My Inventions*. Hart Brothers, 1982.

Articles

Lawren, Bill. "Rediscovering Tesla." *Omni* 10 (March 1988).
Hall, Stephen. "Tesla: A Scientific Saint, Wizard or Carnival Sideman?" *Smithsonian* 17 (June 1986).
Marshall, Eliot. "Seeking Redress for Nikola Tesla." *Science* 214 (October 30, 1981).
Quinby, E. J. "The Life and Times of Nikola Tesla." *Radio Electronics* 54 (August 1983).
Schunaman, Fred. "Nikola Tesla." *Radio Electronics* 51 (October 1980).
Scientific American, 1901 ed., s.v. "Tesla's Wireless Light."
Shapiro, Neil. "Happy Birthday, Tesla." *Popular Mechanics* 156 (July 1981).
———. "The Marconi Controversy." *Popular Mechanics* 156 (July 1981).
———. "Taming the Lightning." *Popular Mechanics* 156 (July 1981).
Wold, Eric. "Simple Tesla Coil." *Radio Electronics* 52 (September 1981).

Index

Photo Acknowledgments

The photographs and illustrations have been reproduced through the courtesy of: pp. 1, 2, 11, 12, 13, 16, 20, 28, 51, 60, 66, 67, 68, 74, 81, 84, 90, 94, 96, 101, 108, 109, 112, 116, 117, 122, 124, 132, 134, 136, 137, Nikola Tesla Museum; pp. 6, 8, 76, 77, 78, 87 (bottom), 102, 130, Nikola Tesla Papers, Rare Book and Manuscript Library, Columbia University; pp. 22, 71, 88, 89, 92, Westinghouse Historical Collection; pp. 35, 57, 63, U.S. Department of the Interior, National Park Service, Edison National Historical Site; pp. 38, 44, Independent Picture Service; pp. 42, 79, 104, The Smithsonian Institution; pp. 46, 126, Bettmann Archive; p. 54, U.S. Immigration and Naturalization Service; pp. 53, 55, 69, 99, 114, Library of Congress; p. 87 (top), Hannibal Convention and Visitors Bureau; p. 131 UPI/Bettmann; p. 137 (inset), copyrighted stamp design reproduced with the permission of the U.S. Postal Service; p. 138, Tesla Memorial Society, Inc. Illustration on p. 18 by Susan Fair Lieber. Diagrams on pp. 36, 37, 50, and 120 by Laura Westlund. Front and back cover photos courtesy of the Nikola Tesla Museum.